~~USES~~

OF THE

HOROSCOPE

Houses

OF THE

Horoscope

BY

Alan Oken

Ibis Press
Lake Worth, Florida

Published in 2009 by Ibis Press
An imprint of Nicolas-Hays, Inc.
P. O. Box 540206
Lake Worth, FL 33454-0206
www.nicolashays.com

Distributed to the trade by
Red Wheel/Weiser, LLC
65 Parker St. • Ste. 7
Newburyport, MA 01950
www.redwheelweiser.com

ISBN 978-089254-156-0

Library of Congress Cataloging-in-Publication Data
Oken, Alan.
Houses of the horoscope / by Alan Oken.
    p. cm.
Originally published: Freedom, Calif. : Crossing Press, c1999.
Includes bibliographical references.
ISBN 978-0-89254-156-0 (alk. paper)
1. Houses (Astrology) I. Title.
BF1716.O38 2009
133.5'3042--dc22   2009032082

Book design by Studio 31.
www.studio31.com

Cover zodiac: Dionysius Freher, from *The Works of Jacob Boehme*
Photo Credit: Harry Smith Archives, photo by Don Snyder.

15 14 13 12 11 10 09
    7   6   5   4   3   2   1

Please note: If you would like to contact Alan Oken, you are welcome to write to
him at alanoken@att.net or visit his website: *www.alanoken.com*

Printed in the United States of America

CONTENTS

For Jean Redman

My dearest friend

*Whose loving support has made
so many years so much more joyful*

Introduction

Astrology is an amazingly accurate tool for better understanding yourself, your friends, your planet, and the nature of Life itself. The natal horoscope is a blueprint and guide that creates a clear map to personal awareness out of the huge mass of astrological data. Calculated for a person's date, time, and place of birth, the natal chart reveals a detailed portrait of an individual's relationship to the world. Its various components reveal who we are, what we have to offer, how we offer it, with whom we are most likely to share our talents, abilities, and love, and so much more.

Astrology is a very complex system of interweaving energies. It takes time and dedication for the student of this ancient science to be able to unravel astrology's symbolic codes and to comprehend its very special language. As the life around us consistently presents us with new challenges to resolve, an increasing number of people have been turning to astrology for the clues, insights, and answers that this special field of study has to offer. I have been a student and practitioner of this cosmic science for more than thirty years, and astrology still amazes and astounds me, surprises and enlightens me, delights and uplifts me. And more—astrology gives me the opportunity to be of service to others.

People who have not studied this subject always approach the astrologer with the same two questions: "How does astrology work?" and "How can the movement of the planets possibly affect our life here on earth?" These queries can be answered in two responses of four simple words each: "The Law of Correspondences," and "As Above, So Below." When we contemplate these two short statements (actually they express the same concept), and open up our minds to their implications, we will have truly expanded our consciousness.

"As Above, So Below" is a famous saying of an ancient legendary sage known historically as "Hermes Trismagistus." This simple statement expresses a metaphysical Law which states that there exists a pattern of Correspondences and relationships in the universe, one that is repeated and reflected in all forms of creation. The distances between the sub-atomic particles contained within the body of an atom, for example, have a similar ratio as the distances between the planets in the solar system, or even the vast spaces between the stars within our own Milky Way galaxy. These sub-atomic particles whirl about their atomic nucleus in the same way as the planets revolve around our Sun and the stars in the Milky Way slowly orbit the galactic center. Astrology is valid because there is no real separation in the universe. Everything and everyone is connected and interconnected. We are One.

The underlying philosophy of astrology accepts this unity of all life. Astrologers are able to apply the meaning of that unity through our awareness of planetary patterns and their reflections of the events of life here on Earth. It is this application of astrology to the more practical side of things that concerns this book. Briefly stated in the astrological vocabulary, the planets answer the question *"What?"*—What is the nature and type of energy expressing itself in your natal chart? The signs refer to *"How?"* –How do these energies reveal themselves? The *"Houses of the Horoscope"* respond to *"Where?"*—Where in your life will this combination of *What* and *How* take place? Example: Mars in Gemini in the 7th House. *What* type of energy is Mars? (Mars is assertive, aggressive, stimulating, and projective.) *How* is Mars making itself known in the person's life? (Gemini deals with communication and mental activity.) *Where* is this taking place for that individual? (The 7th House has to do with partnerships in general and marriage in particular). Thus my interpretation for Mars in Gemini in the 7th House could be summarized as follows: "This individual will tend to be assertive in his communications with his partners. He will tend to stimulate conversations and mental activities in relationships."

Astrology is an ancient science that concerns itself primarily with bringing the heavens above down to our doorstep below. It is by peering through the windows of the *"Houses of the Horoscope"* of the natal chart, that we come to see ourselves as men and women living out our normal lives within the body of a very supernormal universe. It is hoped that this book will help the reader to deepen his or her knowledge of astrology, so that this relationship between heaven and earth may become a more tangible reality.

Alan Oken
Lisbon, Portugal
March 2009

What Are the
Astrological Houses?

Everything in the universe is energy, expressing itself in many qualities, shapes, and forms. The natal horoscope may only be a two-dimensional diagram printed on a three-dimensional piece of paper, but it brings us to understand the multidimensional universe in which we live, and puts us in touch with the life energy of which we (and the cosmos) are composed. The horoscope is an illustration of the *what, how,* and *where* of our life. We can say that the "what" is represented by the planets in our chart. The planets tell us "what" particular type of energy is at work. In studying the planets in our natal map, "what" part or parts of ourselves are we examining? Is it our aggressive and assertive energy (Mars), our instinctual and subconscious energy (Moon), or the vital energy of the life principle itself (Sun)? The signs of the zodiac tell us "how" the energies of the planets are being expressed. Is the assertive part of our nature coming forth into our immediate environment boldly (Mars in Aries), timidly (Mars in Cancer), expansively (Mars in Sagittarius), or unpredictably (Mars in Aquarius)? We could also say that a sign is to a planet what an adverb is to a verb: It describes or modifies the action taking place.

To complete our picture of how the various energies of our life reveal our character and destiny, we have to look at "where" these cosmic energies land. Of course, they land on earth: *where* they land—in which sphere of our life's activities they most strongly express their nature—is revealed by the astrological houses. Understanding the complex nature of the horoscope's house structure is essential to our appreciation of how we function in our daily life.

Let us say that you are a person born in late April with the Sun in Taurus. When a man or a woman is born in the sign of the Bull, the life message is clear: This is an individual who has come to earth to learn about the real values of life. Such values may take a material or monetary form, but external financial considerations may also be a test—a veil which the Taurean has to pierce in order to understand his or her true self-worth. The *house position* of the Taurus Sun will reveal *where* in one's life such lessons are most likely to occur. If the Sun is in the Ninth House, or example, this particular Child of the Bull would most likely uncover her real life values through higher learning, publishing, and achieving a practical philosophy of life. If the Taurus Sun were in the Eleventh House, this person would be much more inclined towards accomplishing his goal of self-awareness through social work, group interactions, and a wide range of friendships. Let us say that you have Mars in Aquarius. Would your rather unpredictable urge for self-assertion most likely express itself

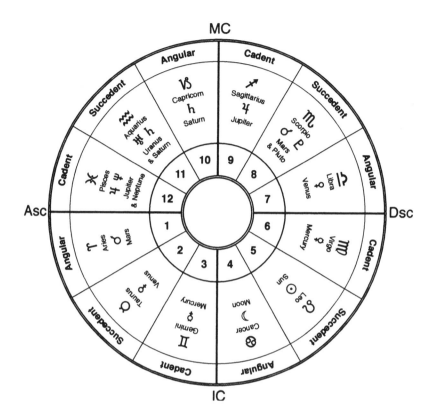

Illustration 1

through your relationships (Seventh House), your career (Tenth House), or in terms of your sexuality (Eighth House)? In effect, the house position tells us "where" on earth Mars is going to land in your life.

A House Divided

Just as we divide the nature of solar energy into the twelve zodiacal types (the sun signs), we also divide the 360 degrees of the wheel of the natal horoscope into twelve houses. This division is based on the date, place, and, especially, time of birth. The date of birth will give the positions of the planets in their signs in the heavens. The place of birth tells the astrologer the longitude and latitude of birth so that this point may be fixed in relationship to the planets. But without the time of birth, the astrologer cannot determine the actual house divisions and anchor the exact relationship between "heaven and earth."

There are any number of methods and systems of house division in current use by astrologers. The differences are based on the way the astrologer chooses to differentiate the heavens into their appropriate sections. Remember that astrology is an art as well as a science, and that the astrologer has a choice in the way he or she interprets the zodiacal "painting." The lines in the heavens, which the astrologer marks on the horoscope to separate the houses, are called the "cusps." Before the advent of computerized astrological software in the late 1970s, all horoscopes had to be mentally calculated, using complex mathematical tables, and then manually drawn upon the wheel. Depending on the astrologer's nationality, generation, and personal preference, one method of house division is usually favored over another. The author, and most other American and many European astrologers born after 1940, generally use what is called the "Placidian system," named after Placidus de Titus, the 17th–century Spanish monk who invented it. Many other astrologers prefer to use the "Koch system," first published in the early 1970s. Neither system works well for births in extreme northern and southern latitudes: Thus, some northern European astrologers like to use the "Equal House method." As this is primarily an introductory text to the meanings of the houses of the horoscope, I will not go into the technical differences between these three and the other half-dozen or so methods of house division in current use. Those readers who are interested in exploring the more mathematical dynamics of the houses are welcome to consult the books recommended for this purpose in the Reference Guide.

All computerized software programs offer a wide variety of house systems: All the modern student of astrology has to do is to push a button, or click a mouse, and the horoscope will be instantly cast, in any method she chooses. It is that simple. Most computerized astrological services, including my own, will send a print-out of a horoscope using the Placidian method, unless otherwise specified by the client. The virtual elimination of the more technical portions of astrological study is a boon, as it allows astrology to be much more accessible to everyone. Yet I still advise serious students of our ancient science (especially those seeking to become professional astrologers) to become familiar with the celestial dynamics of house division, so that the horoscope may be seen inside of your head as a living sphere, and not as a flat series of circles and lines on a piece of paper.

In June of 1970, I met an old swami from Madras, India, who asked me to do his horoscope. I was very young at the time, and just beginning to practice astrology professionally. The request from this venerable holy man took me somewhat aback. With great hesitation, I asked the gentleman, "How can I read for you sir, when the astrological system that I use is so much different from the Hindu system of your country?" "My son," he replied, "the universe is a single image but we all look at it through different lenses. Now you look at my horoscope through your lens and tell me what you see."

No matter what system, no matter which lens you may come to favor, all the house cusps of the chart will be calculated from the "Midheaven," also called the Medium Coeli, the Tenth House cusp, or, most commonly, the MC. If a person in the northern hemisphere is facing due south at the time of birth, the MC corresponds to the point that is directly overhead in the sky. This point will correspond to a degree in the zodiac of the twelve astrological signs. The point of the horizon exactly to your east would correspond to the degree of the zodiac called your "Ascendant," the degree of your rising sign. The cross made by your MC and its opposite point, the IC (Immum Coeli or Fourth House cusp), and the Ascendant (First House cusp) and its opposite point, the Descendant (Seventh House cusp), is the same for all systems of house division. It is only the "intermediary cusps" of the houses that differ, but these differences are important, because they can change the house position of the planets in your chart!

What to do when the time of birth is unknown?

As the degree of the sign on the Midheaven changes approximately every four minutes (one sign every two hours, all twelve signs in the space of a full 24-hour day), the exact time of birth is very important. A few minutes' variation does not matter much for most interpretive purposes, if the signs on the house cusps (especially the four major house cusps) do not change. But the exact time of birth is very important for many methods of astrological predictive work. A variation of more than four minutes in the time of birth is most important, if this time difference will change the Midheaven or the Ascendant. A 4:06 PM birth may give a chart with 29° Aries rising but a 4:10 PM birth time for that same individual would yield a 0° Taurus Ascendant.

Most people born in American or Canadian hospitals after the end of the Second World War will have the time of birth recorded on their official birth certificates. In the large majority of cases, this is the document you have, or your family has. In some cases, however, only the official birth certificate contains this important piece of information; the birth time is not stated on the document handed to the parents when they leave the hospital. An official certificate of birth, with the time of birth, has been recorded (Hospitals hold these for many decades, depending on the laws of their locale). When this time limit is passed, or if the hospital no longer exists, such records are transferred to an office in the hall of records in the county of birth. Birth times are often officially recorded (and many times appear on the family's copy of the birth certificate) in the United Kingdom, Australia, Scandinavian countries, and many other countries of Western Europe. Sometimes birth times go unrecorded or are lost: An individual is then left without this knowledge, or with the vague notion that she was born "some time after lunch," or "just before your father came home from work."

There are three recourses for an individual without a proper birth time.

1. A "Solar Chart" is cast. This is a simple process by which the 360 degrees of the wheel are divided into twelve equal parts of 300. The Sun is placed at the Ascendant, and its degree becomes the one used for all the twelve house cusps. Thus, if one were born on January 13, 1968, the Sun would be at 22° Capricorn. This then becomes the Ascendant. The Second House cusp is thus 22° Aquarius, the Third House cusp is 22° Pisces, the Fourth is 22° Aries, and so on, around the entire wheel. The positions of the planets are calculated for sunrise on the day of birth and put into the chart accordingly. Using a computerized software program makes this step a snap.

2. A "Natural Chart" is constructed. This is an even simpler process that does not require a computer. You will need an ephemeris—a book found in any astrological book shop and some libraries. An ephemeris shows the positions of the planets on any given day of any given year. Divide the Natural Chart into twelve equal parts, placing 0° Aries (the first degree of the zodiac) on the cusp of the First House, 0° Taurus on the Second, 0° Gemini on the Third, and onwards around the wheel, along the natural order of the signs. The planets can then be entered into the house by either their noon or midnight positions on the day of birth, depending on the type of ephemeris you have.

Solar and Natural Charts will yield only very approximate horoscopes, but at least you will have some idea of the relative positions of the planets in your chart, and this is a good place to begin to understand the nature of your birth map. As your knowledge of astrology increases and you get the "feel" of the signs, planets, and houses, you can experiment with the house positions of the planets, based on the events of your life and the nature of your personality. Astrology's main purpose is, after all, the development of an ever increasing and expanding sense of oneself in relation to the cosmos.

If, however, you do not have the birth time and you want an accurate horoscope cast, you need to use the third method: This can only be accomplished by a small handful of the most advanced astrologers. This is called:

3. The "Rectification of the Birth Chart." You will need to prepare a list of at least fifteen to twenty of the most important events in your life, for which you have an accurate and verifiable date (and, if possible, a time). These events may have been very positive or very traumatic, but they must have deep significance and meaning in your life. Such incidents may include the dates (and times) of marriages, deaths of loved ones, births of children or other siblings, changes in residence (or the destruction of a home), accidents or operations, graduations from a university, major shifts in profession, or even the day when you purchased that winning lottery ticket (but not the day when you bought a ticket that lost). It is also a good idea to present the astrologer with photos of yourself at different stages of life, because one's physical appearance is very much indicated by the rising sign, planets in the First House, or other planets that make tight geometrical angles ("aspects") to the Ascendant. Once the astrologer has determined your rising sign, he or she has also determined your birth time within a couple of hours and the first major hurdle to determine your birth sign is over. I am very much against some people who use a pendulum to find out the degree rising in the birth chart or who have other "psychic impressions" that reveal this information. Such methods need to be substantiated by solid techniques of astrological rectification. Even then, the experienced astrologer will ask the client to "live and work" with his or her chart (giving them guidelines as to how to do this) for six months or a year and then to report back for some "fine tuning." In the right hands, a correct rectification can be accomplished and is a worthwhile investment to make if you want to have an accurate birth chart for the rest of your life.

The Name, Address, and Quality of a House

No matter which of the house systems you decide to use, the natal horoscope will always consist of twelve houses. Each of these celestial domiciles corresponds to a number of activities, life circumstances, types of people, objects, and ideas. These are gathered together under a collective keyword phrase that makes the entire contents of the house easy to categorize and remember. These key words are a convenient way to represent the major concept underlying the particular influence of each house, but by no means do they express the entire range of influence of each of these twelve divisions of the natal chart. The twelve house names are as follows:

First House:	House of Self-Image
Second House:	House of Money & Self-Worth
Third House:	House of Communication & Travel
Fourth House:	House of Family & Psychological Roots
Fifth House:	House of Creativity & Pleasure

Sixth House: House of Health & Work
Seventh House: House of Partnership & Marriage
Eighth House: House of Death & Sexuality
Ninth House: House of Higher Education & Philosophy
Tenth House: House of Career & Honor
Eleventh House: House of Organizations & Groups
Twelfth House: House of Secrets

Just as there are several basic groupings into which the signs of the zodiac are categorized[1], there are four hemispheres and four quadrants where a house may have its astrological "address." In addition, there are three major "qualities" into which the houses of the horoscope may be classified. Let us briefly take a look at these eleven various house particulars, in order to familiarize ourselves with the overall nature of how the houses are viewed in the natal chart.

The Four Hemispheres

As you can see from Illustration 2, the houses are divided by two primary lines, creating the major divisions of the chart by hemispheres. This circle of the houses should also be seen as representing the 24 hours of the day. The East/West axis is the horizon line, with the East point (Ascendant) representing sunrise and the West point (Descendant) representing sunset. The people who named these divisions lived north of the Equator. They called the South/Midheaven the "uppermost" point of the horoscope, because when they looked at

---

1 Please see my book, *Alan Oken's Complete Astrology* (published by Ibis Press).

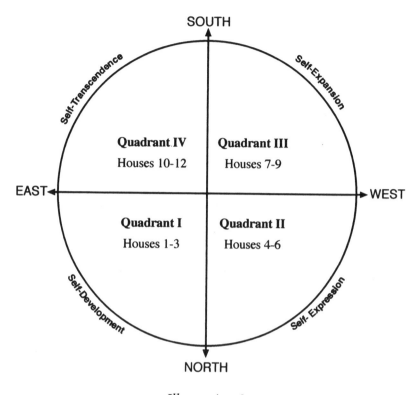

Illustration 2

the noon sun, they were always facing south. (If you stood at the equator, the noon sun would be directly overhead; in the Southern Hemisphere, it is always north of the observer.) The North/Immum Coeli is the lowest point of the chart and can be said to represent midnight.

Southern Hemisphere (Houses 7–12):

These are known as the "social" or "collective" houses. They deal with those aspects of our life that involve the world outside of our inner, personal life. Activities in these domiciles create opportunities for us to interact with the larger world around us. We could also say that this is the *objective* hemisphere of the chart. The Ninth House, for example, is the area in the horoscope that indicates international travel and higher education.

Northern Hemisphere (Houses 1–6):
Astrologers view these sections of the chart as the "personal" area of life. In this portion of the horoscope we find those life situations that affect our personal, psychological development and create in us a sense of separate, individual identity. Another name for this region is the *subjective* hemisphere of the chart. The Third House of the chart, for example, tells the astrologer about a person's immediate environmental circumstances and indicates a person's early education.

Eastern Hemisphere (Houses 10–3):
This is the projective side of the chart. When planets are placed in these six houses, they tend to assert their energy. People with a majority of their planetary powers in this area of the horoscope are said to be very much involved with asserting themselves in life and opening their own doors. This would be especially true if the planets were found in the First and/or Tenth House. Mars (assertion) in the Tenth House (career), for example, can be an excellent placement for someone who really wants to get ahead in life.

Western Hemisphere (Houses 4–9):
This is the responsive side of the chart. When planets are placed in these six houses, they tend to respond to life situations that are already in motion. The Moon (emotions) in the Seventh House (relationships), for example, is a very good

placement for a teacher or counselor: It indicates a person who can respond to other people's emotional needs. People with the majority of their planets in these houses would be very likely to wait for an invitation to a party; Eastern Hemisphere people could just as easily invite themselves!

The Four Quadrants

When we combine the influences of the hemispheres we have the quadrants:

I. Northeast (Houses 1–3):
Quadrant of Personal Identity. This is the most personal of the four quadrants, indicating one's physical body and personality temperament (First House); one's material possessions, attitude to money, and basic life values (Second House); and one's mind, ability to communicate, and natural communication skills (Third House).

II. Northwest (Houses 4–6):
Quadrant of Personal Expression. Having established the sense of personal identity in Quadrant I, the individual may now move forward to express himself or herself a bit further. This is done through the shaping of a more individualized identity. The basis for this is located through one's family and early psychological development (Fourth House). It is extended through one's relationship to one's children and one's creative interests (Fifth House). It is made practical through one's job, skills, and ways of improving oneself (Sixth House).

III. Southwest (Houses 7–9):

Quadrant of Social Identity. The third quadrant of the chart leads to greater self-expansion. This is the social area of life, one in which we find our most important relationships and life partner (Seventh House). It is also the area of the horoscope that deals with one of the most complex issues of life—our sexuality (Eighth House). The Eighth is also called the "House of Death" as both death and sexuality are two facets of a much larger Eighth House issue—transformation. We are also expanded through our university education and foreign travel (Ninth House).

IV. Southeast (Houses 10–12):

Quadrant of Social Expression. The final Quadrant of the horoscope could also be termed the universal region of life. It is here that one learns that one is more than just an individual ego, out in the world working to satisfy its own needs and desires. It is through the Tenth House that we come into the larger world, and if it is our nature to do so (for not all people have "strong" Tenth House placements), stand before the public as an authority in our field. The Eleventh House brings to us the opportunity to interact with social groups, organizations, and humanitarian causes that help us learn about service to humanity. The Twelfth House is the most mysterious. It speaks about things hidden to us—hidden enemies and hidden friends, hidden talents and resources, and those subtle (and not so subtle!) ways that we bring harm into our own lives. The Twelfth House also opens us to the more spiritual side of life.

The Angular Houses

If you refer back to Illustrations 1 and 2, you will see that the Angular Houses correspond to the Cardinal Signs and to the beginnings of the cusps of the four quadrants. The First House begins with the Ascendant (East) and the sign Aries/Spring, the Fourth with the IC (North) and the sign Cancer/Summer, the Seventh with the Descendant (West) and the sign Libra/Fall, and the Tenth with the Midheaven (South) and the sign Capricorn/Winter. The cardinal signs are indicative of new beginnings and the generation of new cycles. They are the signs that occur at the beginning of the four seasons, and they usher in those activities which correspond to the major climatic and psychological divisions of the earth's yearly cycle.

The Angular Houses are said to be the most important in the horoscope: When planets are placed in these four positions in your natal horoscope, their activity is the most apparent and tends to dominate the direction of your life. The entire structure of the horoscope is based on the nature of these four angles. In most (but not all) cases, the other eight houses will supplement and support the "story" told by the four angles. When astrologers examine a chart to forecast events affecting a person or a nation, we examine when planets in the heavens cross any of these four angles. Such crossings ("transits") are very noteworthy indeed!

Just as the four seasons may be seen as two pairs—spring and fall, summer and winter—so do we also tend to see these angular houses (and all the other houses) in terms of pairs.

First House/Seventh House:

If the First House tends to describe "me" and my relationship to myself, the Seventh House will describe "you" and my relationship to you. In other words, the First/Seventh House axis is the one most involved with my relationship with others. It speaks about myself and what I am seeking to complete in myself by having a relationship with "you," i.e., with other people. As most people seek self-fulfillment through their relationships, the nature of this important interchange is revealed by the particulars of this Ascendant/Descendant axis.

Fourth House/Tenth House:

The Fourth House reveals much about one's psychological foundations and family background. The Tenth speaks about what one sets out to accomplish in the world. If we look at the Fourth/Tenth House axis as a sort of family tree, we could say that the Fourth House speaks about one's "roots," while the Tenth reveals one's "fruits." If my roots have been well watered and well nourished, then the world can expect healthy produce. If, however, there has been trauma to the roots, then the fruits will be stunted.

The Succedent Houses

The Succedent Houses correspond to the Fixed Signs and represent the midpoints of the four quadrants. If we maintain our analogy to the four seasons, we will find that the fixed signs anchor the energy of these primary divisions of the year: Taurus/ Second House/Spring; Leo/Fifth House/ Summer; Scorpio/Eighth House/Fall; and Aquarius/Eleventh House/Winter. The fixed signs focus, strengthen, and define the nature of each of the four seasons. In a similar way, we can say that the Succedent Houses anchor the nature of each of the four quadrants. They develop the essential nature of the angular positions, adding *definition* and values to our sense of self.

The Succedent Houses are the storehouses of the horoscope—they hold our treasures and act as bank accounts or safety-deposit boxes, where we go to store what we value or to withdraw our valuables when we have need of them. Planets in any of these houses tend either to augment or deny, support or sabotage what we value in ourselves, others, and life in general. Thus, depending on the entire nature of the horoscope, the Succedent Houses have the ability to sustain (or inhibit) our urges for self-development and personal achievement.

Second House/Eighth House:
The Second House speaks about what I hold dear to me my personal possessions, values, and material goods. It preserves and gives physical form to my sense of self (First House/ Ascendant). Its opposite, the Eighth House, is the "House of Death": It speaks about the destruction of form, only, as a vehicle of transformation so that more refined forms may evolve. As the *second house from the Seventh,* the Eighth House also says much about other people's resources and values, especially those owned or possessed by my partner.

Fifth House/Eleventh House:
Creative expression—of myself and my sense of my own self-worth (Second House)—is very much the province of the Fifth House of the horoscope. We are still in the realm of the "personal houses," and the most personal of all creations are my children. The Eleventh House, however, describes those creative activities which are much more impersonal and collective in nature and orientation. Thus, planning a dinner party for my immediate family and intimate friends is a very Fifth House activity; organizing a public event for a charitable cause with a group of associates is more in the realm of the "social houses," and hence an Eleventh House activity.

The Cadent Houses

The Cadent Houses are related to those times of year that usher in the changes in our yearly cycle. They are thus connected to the Mutable Signs of the zodiac and the last month of each of the seasons: Gemini/Third House/Spring; Virgo/Sixth House/Summer; Sagittarius/Ninth House/Fall; and Pisces/Twelfth House/Winter. The mutable signs create the opportunity for the *interplay* and *exchange* of the various elements in nature. They serve as *links* and *connections* between people, ideas, places, and objects.

In a similar way, the Cadent Houses indicate those experiences and opportunities in life that allow us to communicate, share, and disseminate our sense of self and our creative abilities. They differentiate and *expand, circulate* and *integrate* who we are and what we have with the world around us; they bring experiences from outside of ourselves into our lives, so that we may grow and develop.

Third House/Ninth House:

These are the two so-called "mental houses" but they indicate two different spheres of mental activity. The Third House is very connected to the way our mind was trained in youth. It speaks about our early education and the ideas and opinions we inherited from our parents and early environment. It is essentially the house of our early education and our "neighborhood" travels. The Ninth House has much more to do with our philosophical and religious approach to life. It speaks about our wider life concepts, those that transcend pure self-interest and personal opinion. It is the house of our higher education, and of travels that take us outside of our homeland.

Sixth House/Twelfth House:

It is in the Sixth House that we have the skills, techniques, and tools to approach our personal life—especially its day-to-day affairs. The Sixth House reveals those processes we use to create our road to self-improvement. In this respect, it is also the house of health and physical culture. The Twelfth House is the most mysterious and least understood of all the astrological "domiciles." It is the place where we have our spiritual tools so that we may approach the life of the Universe. It speaks to us about our spiritual health and our "inner gifts," and about as those methods, habits, and addictions we have harm or "undo" us.

Summary

The first three houses are specifically oriented to the expression of oneself: the First House inducts one's immediate approach to life, the Second constitutes one's personal wealth and values, while the Third reveals one's natural way of thinking and communicating. The next grouping of three houses involve relationships based on the family, and one's psychological foundation in life, as signified by the Fourth House. The Fifth represents the fruit of the family and that foundation, namely, one's children or other expressions of one's creativity. The Sixth House speaks about those jobs that are necessary to support oneself and one's family, and about those social connections directly connected to the family, such as employees or pets. The next group of three houses is based upon social interrelationship, with its foundation in marriage or other forms of intimate partnership (Seventh House). The Eighth House shares the fruits of those relationships and reveals the potential for regeneration and, consequently, greater growth. The Ninth House reveals one's approach to understanding the underlying legal and philosophical concepts upon which the larger structures of society are built. The last three houses are the most impersonal of all: They involve the integration of the individual's identity and creative efforts into the great human collective. The Tenth House signifies one's professional contribution to society, and the status one achieves accordingly. The Eleventh House is more concerned with group intent and collective endeavor, and is therefore the house of friends and of organizations to which we may belong. The Twelfth House is the location for our hidden talents, treasures, and resources, and for those forces of our personality that embody our own urge for self-undoing. The Twelfth is the hardest house to understand, for within it are contained some of our deepest secrets—factors in our life that either prove to be our greatest gifts or our worst enemies.

I Am Myself

The Ascendant/Rising Sign and the contents of the First House yield a great deal of information, about who we are to ourselves, and about the image we project to others. It is the projection of our self-image, the door through which we express and activate our inner motivations and instinctual psychological needs. The sign on the Ascendant reveals our relationship with our immediate environment, and our physical appearance and body type. It is also the point in the horoscope that mirrors the first impression a person is likely to make in any social situation.

If you were to spend your life in a glass house and all of the glass were tinted blue, no matter what the insides of your house looked like (your rugs, your furniture, etc.), people looking in at you would see you and everything around you with a blue tint. In the same way, your perception of the world outside of your blue glass house would be colored by this same tint. Stepping outside of one's house is very difficult, for we tend to take the particular coloration of our personality wherever we go, and to project its hue on everyone we meet. The study of astrology (including other people's horoscopes) can make this voyage into the objective world a lot easier and a great deal more interesting.

Signs on the Cusp of the First House

The following paragraphs will give basic indications of the nature of each sign, when it is rising in the chart.

A person's initial approach to life—the Ascendant—is modified through the sign:

Aries as an urgent need to express oneself through a constant self-projection upon the immediate environment. An individual with Aries rising often reacts instinctively to any given stimulus or challenge, with an overly enthusiastic attitude or with undue haste. The Ram on the Ascendant does indeed describe an eager and often brave individual, but also one who may not see the larger, overall picture of what lies in front of his impetuous nose. He is very confrontational by nature and a defender of injustice. Aries rising often needs to learn how to balance his incessant urge to plunge forward and conquer; he can achieve that balance by using a more delicate and diplomatic hand. This placement usually indicates an ability to succeed in life when the goals are short-term and immediate. Life is very quick for Aries rising, and patience with oneself and others often has to be cultivated. However, Aries will rise up to action when most others fall behind.

Taurus as a need to achieve some form of concrete and material success through one's efforts. No matter what the inner motivations may be or the degree of urgency, Taurus rising will react with caution and circumspection to the circumstances in her environment. Material and financial considerations are of major concern once she has decided to use her personal energy towards the achievement of any goal. Taurus rising tends to be slow and deliberate in her approach to life. When this sign is on the Ascendant of the horoscope, it is known to endow a person with great physical magnetism and often with considerable beauty as well. As Taurus is a sign of Venus, there is a distinct sensual nature, and an appreciation for all of the arts. Taurus is not quick to commit herself, and she may find that she can be reluctant and apprehensive when approaching new and untried circumstances. Determination and a strong will (sometimes expressed as stubbornness and willfulness!) are other characteristics of this sign, when on the cusp of the First House.

Gemini with the ability to express oneself in life in a great variety of ways. A person with Gemini on the cusp of the First House has an inborn sense of versatility and a constant need to change his environment. This gives rise to a loathing of routine, a love of movement and, consequently, to the cultivation of a great many fascinating and interconnected life experiences. At the same time, Gemini rising may also lead to a superficial attitude, and an approach to one's goals that results in a dissipation of creative energy and the scattering of one's achievements. A person with the Twins on the Ascendant is usually slender, nervous, and quick of step, and will enjoy changing his appearance frequently. Duality is an underlying theme of his life and a Gemini Ascendant frequently finds that he is walking down two paths simultaneously. Gemini rising is a natural-born communicator, and is at his best when linking people together for mutually beneficial plans and projects.

Cancer by a keen sense of self-preservation. The sensitivity of this sign leads to an extremely sympathetic and understanding nature, but there is often an overriding tendency to take all initial impressions and life circumstances too personally. Unless it is conditioned by other circumstances in the horoscope, this Ascendant can give an overly subjective approach to life. The initial drive is focused on securing a foundation or "home base," from which all outer activities may safely proceed. Once Cancer rising feels firm and whole within herself, she then becomes an extremely nurturing and generous person, always available to bring comfort and nourishment to those in her immediate environment, and beyond. Emotional insecurity will be Cancer rising's constant nemesis, until such time as fears and apprehensions are replaced with clear thinking and unselfish actions.

Leo in an often grandiose and sometimes exaggerated manner, as there is a tendency towards self-dramatization. Leo rising is keenly aware of life as a stage, and he is often at its center. A Leo Ascendant gives the ability to organize oneself and others efficiently. It bestows enormous creative potential as well as a love and appreciation of children. Like a child, Leo rising needs to be appreciated and strives to cultivate a high "approval rating" among his friends and colleagues. Leo on the cusp of the First House usually imparts a proud, handsome appearance. The Lion loves to dress up for any occasion. He possesses a great liking for clothes, jewelry, and accessories, and pays a great deal of attention to his hair. There is a strong attraction to the "good life," along with a very powerful romantic nature. Leo rising's favorite pastime is the pursuit of pleasure and leisure.

Virgo as a distinct awareness of the many details of life in her immediate surroundings. A Virgo Ascendant indicates a person who is extremely fastidious in the image she presents to the world. On the other hand, many people with Virgo rising get so lost in the details of life, and in all the "shoulds" and "shouldn'ts," that neatness and organization become impossible to achieve, much less maintain. Virgo on the First House cusp bestows a highly practical approach to life, in which one's job and finances will always be a major factor in all decision-making. Many people with Virgo rising have developed service into a graceful art, and are ever eager to be of help to others. They also possess a deep resourcefulness which allows them to come up with amazing solutions to life's many challenges.

Libra by a continuous attempt to bring harmony and balance into their environment. A Libra Ascendant gives the need for a great many social contacts. When this sign is on the First House cusp of a chart, it indicates an individual who tends to see himself through the eyes and reactions of others. In this respect, Libra rising must take care not to compromise his own sense of individuality through a codependent need for constant cooperation from the people in his immediate circle. Libra rising is often accompanied by considerable physical beauty, grace, and charm. The urge to please dominates the life—there is certainly the urge not to displease. This sometimes exaggerated concern with being judged as a "bad guy" can lead to tremendous vacillation and indecisiveness (and this tendency can indeed be the cause of problems in Libra rising relationships). Libra, like Taurus, is one of Venus' signs; therefore, the arts and the creation of beauty are very important to the Scales.

Scorpio with a definite degree of self-control and a distinct reticence about revealing oneself. Scorpio rising is known to have "eagle eyes." There is definitely a piercing gaze but, in addition to this distinct physical characteristic, this Ascendant is also capable of seeing what lies beyond the surface appearance of people. Scorpio rising's eyes peer into the core of one's emotions, probing deeply into one's innermost feelings. When the eagle is flying high, Scorpio can use this sensitivity as a helpful, supportive, and transformational healing tool. The earthbound Scorpion, however, may use this perception to dominate another person, and can be quite emotionally deceptive. All Scorpio risings are very aware of the sexual energy in their environment. This awareness can be very challenging to those of this sign who are not themselves sexually integrated and balanced.

Sagittarius as a tendency towards exuberance and expansiveness. A Sagittarius Ascendant gives a person the need to cover a great deal of territory. These are the philosophers of the zodiac and they possess a distinct urge to travel, learn, teach, and just experience what life has to offer. In this respect, Sagittarius rising can indicate a definite physical, emotional, and intellectual restlessness. Life is seen as a challenge, a battle to be overcome with optimism and self-assurance. The need for a distinct life purpose is uppermost, and it is only when he is without a clear target for his arrows that the Centaur-Archer may be perceived as troubled. When Sagittarius is on the cusp of the First House, the individual tries to avoid all circumstances that tend to limit his personal spontaneity. He is basically an independent person and has a distinct disdain for any form of imposed restrictions on his behavior. The need to cultivate correct personal responsibility is frequently a test with this rising sign.

Capricorn in a self-restrained manner. This Ascendant imparts constraints on any form of impulsive activity, because there is a distinct need to project a "good" image into the environment. There is also a need to maintain and sustain this image, building upon it rather than changing it. Capricorn on the First House cusp of the natal chart can develop into a very restrictive influence. Yet, when used objectively and wisely, the risen energies of the Mountain Goat can give the steadfastness that leads to great achievement, and the ability to overcome conflicting and challenging environmental circumstances. Capricorn rising bestows the ability to see life from a lofty perspective, giving long-range vision, patience, and insight. Duty, tradition, and responsibility to self and others are all very important to this sign, and strongly condition this person's attitude to relationships.

Aquarius by a desire to express oneself in a highly original way. There is a definite love/hate relationship with groups and organizations. On the one hand, Aquarius on the Ascendant indicates a person who is markedly individualistic, and who finds it absolutely necessary to be his own person, in his own way. On the other hand, there is a distinct calling towards idealistic thinking and humanitarian efforts that require group interaction and a high degree of social participation. Some Aquarians will make sure that they individualize themselves through a hobby, pastime, or habit pattern that places them apart from others, in action and/or appearance. Other Water Bearers will join a group, cult, or organization whose collective orientation marks the individual with a special identity. Aquarius rising is acutely aware of any and all communication possibilities. They are natural networkers but must take care not to overextend themselves and thereby lose their connection to their center.

Pisces by an extremely impressionable and sensitive nature. Pisces rising is drawn to environments provide a constant source of emotional stimulation. In those milieus, they can express themselves through the many avenues and channels that they feel are open to them. This is a sign of great duality: often, when this sign is on the Ascendant, it also indicates people who have a need to withdraw! Individuals with Pisces on First House cusp can be so absorptive that they must find a place of peace and solitude, so that they can "ring out the sponge" of their intense impressions. When this is creatively expressed, Pisces rising individuals become artists, mystics, and healers. Their ability to identity with everyone gives them a distinctly universal and compassionate nature. Yet many rising Fish swim downstream. It is then that this sign indicates a person intent upon their own self-undoing through addictions and habits that dissolve the personality into a pool of undifferentiated emotions.

Planets in the First House[2]

The Sun in the First House gives the impulse to project oneself continuously into the immediate environment. In this way, the individual becomes the dominating force in any set of life circumstances in which she finds herself. There is a tendency towards a general optimism and a "sunny" disposition about life. Care has to be taken that the drive to be the center of attention at all times does not become the overwhelming personality characteristic of one's life.

The Moon in the First House reveals a strong need to be appreciated by everyone with whom the individual comes into contact. There is also great sensitivity to one's personal safety and security—physical and emotional. This, if not modified, can lead to an overly self-protective nature. Here is

---

2 The following paragraphs (and all other paragraphs under this heading in the following sections) give the reader the essential meanings of the planets when in the various astrological domiciles. A complete explanation of all the indications of planetary placements is beyond the scope of this project. You will come across such phrases as "when well placed, if afflicted, when in relationship to the other planets," etc. These words refer to the position of the planets in the various signs, and in geometrical relationship ("aspects") to the other planets. *Pocket Guide to the Astrological Houses* is a handy reference and will indeed point the reader in the direction of understanding planetary placements. For a more detailed study of the subject, please refer to the Reference Guide at the end of this book.

a person who seeks to care for everyone in his environment, but also expects to be taken care of, in return. The home environment will be a very important factor in his life.

Mercury in the First House indicates a strong intellectual approach to life and a need for constant communication of one's ideas and opinions. It is often an indication of a nervous or high-strung individual, a restless person with a great need for movement and change.

Venus in the First House gives charm and grace as well as a considerable degree of personal magnetism. There is a distinct love of beauty and the arts, and a tendency to be sensually lazy, with a distinct urge to give and receive pleasure.

Mars in the First House speaks about a fearless and aggressive nature, a person who needs to dominate his immediate environment through a sense of distinct territoriality. It is a position that gives drive, determination, and the ability to recuperate after any setback or loss.

Jupiter in the First House denotes a generous and buoyant approach to life. This is a person who has to do everything in a big way, so much so that natural exuberance can easily give way to an overblown sense of self-importance. These are large people, in every sense of the word.

Saturn in the First House often bestows a self-repressed nature with a tendency towards the melancholic. This position of Saturn imparts a need to deal with the realities of life at a very early age. Such conditioning can lead either to a deeply wise and responsible individual or to a person who, having missed out on childhood, grows up to be an adult child ever in search of what she or he lost.

Uranus in the First House gives the tendency to be highly individualistic, spontaneous, and irreverent about other people's ways of doing things. This is a person whose life is unpredictably full of surprises and who is also unpredictably surprising!

Neptune in the First House creates a veil of mystery around a person, one that gives the individual a strange allure and attractiveness. Compassion, and great sensitivity, accompany this position; so does an attraction for the arts and all things considered spiritual. Care must be taken, however, as Neptune here may also indicate a life that tends to become lost in glamour and self-deceit—the veil then becomes a shroud.

Pluto in the First House indicates a loner, a person who is constantly undergoing deep transformational experiences. This powerful position adds intensity and depth to one's nature, and can be a very potent and positive force for bringing healing and renewal into any set of circumstances. Life is filled with definite endings and new beginnings that are directly related to one's inner growth and development.

First House People, Places, and Things

Astrological Factors
  Quality: Angular
  Quadrant: Northeast
  Natural Sign Ruler: Aries
  Natural Planetary Ruler: Mars

People
  Paternal aunts and uncles
  Maternal grandfather
  Paternal grandmother

Places and Things
  Myself and my relationship to the environment
  Personality and projected image
  The (initial) effects we have on others
  Physical appearancem especially head, face, nose, and eyes
  Complexion and outstanding physical characteristics
  Habits and personal interests
  General outlook on life
  Childhood and early envirnomental circumstances

I Am My Values and Resources

We have seen that the First House establishes and defines our sense of self—our ego in its moment-to-moment contact with the environment. The Second House fleshes out our individuality, giving it greater form, substance, and support. In this respect, the Second House should be considered our bank. It holds our material goods and our attitudes to what we own. On the most basic, physical level, this is the house of our money, personal riches, and possessions. It tells us about our attitude towards money—how we acquire it, how we spend it, and even how much of this precious substance we are likely to have in our lives. Through a careful examination of the Second House, an astrologer can see your earning and spending capacities, and gain insight into the way you handle your financial responsibilities.

This astrological domicile also describes a great deal about our self-worth, self-esteem, and sense of personal values. What we earn in life, and the way we deal with all that is material, have a lot to do with the sign on the cusp of this house, and with any planets that are placed within the house. Planet and sign, when applied to the nature of the Second House, will show us how we may develop our sense of self-worth in order to refine our relationship to money (and to our desire nature in general). These two factors will also reveal what may inhibit or impede our material growth and prosperity.

Signs on the Cusp of the Second House

The relationship we have to the material factors of life, and to our sense of self-worth, is modified in the Second House by the sign:

Aries in a highly individualistic way. This often expresses itself as a strong urge to live up to the challenges of proving oneself in the material world. The way to success has many starts and stops, as well as a tendency to over-idealize one's concepts. But this is a "never say die" sign, and Aries on this cusp will not rest until personal victory is achieved. Aries here may indicate a tendency to spend money on impulsive whims; sometimes this is money that one doesn't have. If this characteristic is not tempered, it can lead to indebtedness.

Taurus through an individual's will to own and hold on to the things of personal value. This sign endows a person with a very powerful urge for comfort and material security. Sometimes the physical desire nature is too strong, leading to a possessive and selfish nature. Yet Taurus can also be a very generous sign when on this cusp, recognizing other people's material needs and helping to supply them.

Gemini as a tendency to earn money in a variety of ways. This sign gives great versatility and the urge to experiment with a number of different modes for expressing one's talents and abilities. The sense of self-worth will be established through experimentation, and there will be ability in a number of different fields. Care has to be taken that the individual is not spending his resources in too many places simultaneously, thereby wasting time, money, and energy.

Cancer through a deep sense of concern about personal nourishment and well-being. Cancer on this cusp seeks to fill its own pantry and ensure the material well-being and comfort of family and close friends. When in the horoscope of a spiritually mature person, this sign/cusp combination indicates a person who intends to feed and nurture all the children of the world. When taken to the opposite extreme, this combination gives rise to a very selfish nature, as a fear of lack predominates one's attitude towards material well being.

Leo through pride in oneself and one's talents and capabilities. Money and material possessions are earned through a very personal, creative sensibility. There is a tendency to a slow but steady progress through life and a gradual growth of one's financial state. People with Leo on this cusp tend to play favorites with their resources. They are generous to a fault with those they esteem and they are penny-pinchers with others. Children, however, will be generously provided for financially.

Virgo through a strictly practical way with finances. When expressed positively, this sign/cusp combination results in a well-organized and tidy attitude toward money and the use of one's talents and abilities. One has a distinctly practical orientation to life and there is a "place for everything and everything has its place." When misapplied, Virgo on this cusp indicates a tendency to be thoroughly disorganized financially, and gives rise to a person who can never keep his accounts or checkbook in order.

Libra as a balanced attitude towards money. The Scales on the cusp of the Second House indicate a person who likes to share. At the very least, one's attitude is: "You give me something of value and I will return something of equal value to you." Money is often acquired through the expression of one's artistic nature. Libra on the Second House cusp has a way with people, which may attract positive financial opportunities. When the Scales are unbalanced, however, this sign/cusp combination indicates a person whose life is like a seesaw, with tremendous financial swings and many ups and downs.

Scorpio with a need to refine or transform our interplay with matter. The Second House expresses our urge to acquire and thereby brings out our desire nature. Scorpio is the sign of the transformation of desires. When this sign is on the cusp, it indicates that an individual faces a major life lesson regarding the right use of money. This usually involves refinement of the desire to own and possess, and a person is given a tremendous sense of personal freedom when the tests of this sign/cusp are successfully passed. In a more practical sense, this sign/cusp speaks about an individual who earns her own resources through dealing with other people's money.

Sagittarius as a generous, carefree, and sometimes reckless attitude towards money. There is a tendency towards speculation and gambling when the Centaur is on this cusp. The individual likes the excitement of the adventure of earning. Winning or losing are all part of the game and it is the game that counts. There is also a natural orientation toward expressing one's talents and abilities through teaching, publishing, and travel. These are the areas in life where one is most likely to find material support.

Capricorn as a careful and cautious approach to the use of personal resources. At the very least, this is the attitude that one must learn to cultivate! One of the basic lessons here is to learn how to respect financial structures and learn how to budget one's resources correctly. Saturn, Capricorn's ruling planet, will dominate the influence of this sign/cusp placement. The message of Saturn is very clear: "Right responsibility towards your own talents and abilities will pay off in the long run. It may take time to cultivate your fortune in life, but do not despair; just keep on climbing the mountain of your personal goals."

Aquarius as an orientation to express one's talents and abilities either in a unique and original way or as part of a group of people working toward the same goal. Circulation of resources is the key to success, when the Water Bearer is on the cusp of the Second House. It will be important for the individual to network with others so that she may participate in a collective effort at earning income. This may be as simple as working at a desk along with hundreds of others at a major corporation, or it may involve the establishment of a specialty boutique on the Worldwide Web. There is often a humanistic approach to the use of one's resources, and it is highly likely that this individual would have a favorite charity or cause, to which she would contribute.

Pisces through a great deal of idealism, faith, and trust. The arts—especially dance, theater, music, and film—may be involved in this person's way of using his or her talents and abilities, for financial returns. When positive, this sign/cusp combination embodies the phrase, "The Universe will provide." There is an abiding faith in life and a knowledge that there is one uniting stream, which allows all resources to flow together. Still, many individuals with Pisces on the Second will believe that "some of these resources will float right to my door." This is true! When negative, there is an urge to swim in "hot water" and to become involved in financial situations that may not be totally legal.

Planets in the Second House

The Sun in the Second House gives the need to make the most out of one's own talents and resources. There is a distinct tendency to create those circumstances which provide opportunities for material security, stability of purpose, and the successful establishment of oneself in the everyday practicalities of life. On the other hand, should the Sun be in a poor position in respect to the other planets,[3] this position can bring about distinct challenges to one's attitude to money and consequent financial position in life.

The Moon in the Second House strives to bring form and focus to the obtaining of those "creature comforts" that make life easier and more pleasant. This position allows one to make the best of whatever one has at hand. There is also the tendency to be very preoccupied and worried when there is a lack of material sustenance, even for a short period of time. This is a likely occurrence (especially in the mutable signs[4]) , as the Moon definitely goes through "phases."

Mercury in the Second House can be excellent for turning ideas into practical life experience that yields financial rewards. Mercury in this position is never at a loss to make the right connections with other people so that individual talents and abilities may be readily communicated and shared. He bestows versatility and adaptability to one's talents and abilities. The sense of personal freedom is closely connected to a person's sense of self-worth, when Mercury is in the Second.

---

3 These relationships, called "planetary aspects," form an important branch of astrology. The reader may consult the author's book, *Alan Oken's Complete Astrology* (Ibis Press), or see the Reference Guide at the end of this book, for a detailed examination of this facet of astrological studies.

4 Gemini, Virgo, Sagittarius, and Pisces.

Venus in the Second House is, more often than not, a very positive influence. She enhances a person's ability to magnetize resources, either in the form of money and other material valuables, or in the form of relationships that can be helpful and supportive. One caution: Venus loves to indulge in sensual pleasures and can indicate waste and sloth.

Mars in the Second House can help a person assert her sense of self-worth and go after her financial and material aims. Mars can also bring discord in this position, through arguments over finances and a desire nature that may be too strong for one's own good.

Jupiter in the Second House is an indicator of good fortune and the potential for great wealth. This is especially true if Jupiter is in Taurus, Cancer, Scorpio, or Capricorn. The individual can use his talents very expansively and can seize upon positive financial opportunities when they come his way—and they do! On the other hand, Jupiter in this position can give a tendency to be very speculative and impractical (especially when in Sagittarius or Leo), leading to large losses. No matter which sign Jupiter is in, when he is in the Second House he never leaves a person empty-handed.

Saturn in the Second House gives lessons in the proper management and budgeting of resources. It is not an indication of financial liquidity or fluidity but in some cases it does indicate inherited wealth. When Saturn is well placed in this house by sign (especially Taurus, Libra, Capricorn, and Aquarius), it can indicate the ability to structure one's resources easily and profitably. It can also indicate having associations and social contacts that aid and support one. When poorly placed in relationship to some of the other planets, it can bring about distinct financial hardships.

Uranus in the Second House indicates that there are sudden changes of fortune in a person's life that come about in the most unexpected ways. Such reversals usually accompany a shift in life attitude toward the use of one's talents and abilities. This can take the form of sudden flashes of insight that make a person abandon what they have taken years to establish and that prove to be quite correct. In any event, Uranus usually acts with suddenness and drama.

Neptune in the Second House can indicate amazing resourcefulness: It is as though the resources of life came suddenly forth, manifesting with the wave of a wand. When Neptune is well placed in this domicile, there is a special protection that allows the individual to drink from the well that is the source of all wealth and riches. When poorly placed in the Second, there is the tendency to waste or misuse resources. In the extreme, this can lead to criminal acts of deception and deceit.

Pluto in the Second House can act as a mine filled with deep veins of gold or other precious substances. It is an incredible regenerator of resources and certainly aids in the recuperation process after any form of loss. This is so, when Pluto is well positioned in the horoscope in this astrological domicile. When Pluto is poorly placed in the Second House, it can completely destroy a person's resources; psychologically, an afflicted Pluto in the Second House is known to create a very profound lack of self-worth.

Second House People, Places, and Things

A. Astrological Factors
Quality: Succedent
Quadrant: Northeast
Natural Sign Ruler: Taurus
Natural Planetary Ruler: Venus

B. People
Friends of the family
Bankers and financial advisors
Land owners

C. Places and Things
My money and personal finances
Sense of personal values, both financial and moral
Personal possessions, especially land, stocks, bonds, and fixtures
Investment potential and attitude toward investing
Orientation to issues of practical security
Situations affecting personal income
Supplies, stores, assets
Debts, gains, losses, profits
Children's profession

THE THIRD HOUSE

I Am My Mind

We could characterize this domicile by saying that it reveals the ways we *relate* to our environment, especially to the people in intimate or early life settings. This is somewhat different than the nature of the Ascendant and the First House, as that important position in the natal chart speaks more about the *impression* we make upon the environment and not so much about the *interactions* that take place within a given social setting. The First House does indeed tell us something about our early life circumstances, but the Third House will go into this area in much greater detail. Learning how to combine First and Third House indications will help to amplify our understanding of a person's early environmental conditioning.

The Third House is also the place in the horoscope where we can discover additional information about our relationships with our siblings. The Third will also describe our brothers and sisters, especially our oldest sibling and/or the one who made the deepest impression on us or on the rest of our family. The Third House also speaks about our neighbors and those friends close enough to be considered as brothers or sisters. The Third House also points to our formative and secondary education and to the teachers we had during that period of our lives.

This is a very busy house: It deals with short journeys, thoughts, opinions, and all types of communication. A "short journey" (in this era of jet travel) is shorter than three days, and is made for purposes of communication. A "short journey" is never a vacation, adventure, or quest. Most importantly, the Third House speaks about the way we use our minds and how we communicate through the written and spoken word.

Signs on the Cusp of the Third House

The way we communicate and formulate our thoughts is modified in the Third House by the sign:

Aries as an urge to be direct in thought and action. There is very little subtlety or subterfuge when Aries is on the cusp of this house. The tendency is to get to the point in conversations and get there as quickly as possible. There is a definite urge for excitement and challenge in travel—in youth, this person made going around the corner to the supermarket into an adventure. This sign/cusp combination usually indicates few, if any, siblings. It can also indicate strong sibling rivalry.

Taurus as a tendency to think things out thoroughly and completely, before making any verbal or written commitment. The early environment was heavily geared to the practical aspects of life, so ways of communicating are now very much involved with material considerations and their consequences. The individual may be reluctant to move about too much, unless he can travel in very comfortable circumstances, or to familiar and secure places.

Gemini as a very active and busy mind. This is the natural sign of the Third House and is usually indicative of a positive influence in the life. The individual is likely to have had several siblings, of whom one in particular was extremely important. There is a great love of movement and learning, but not necessarily in a one-pointed direction. They tend to be interested in a lot of things and to be able to create many mental associations and connections. A good indication for work in the areas of communications and the media.

Cancer as a person who was strongly affected, for good or ill (depending on other factors in the chart), by her early environment. Sentimentality, and nostalgia for the past, may be strong components of the personality. Very often this person acted like a parent to her siblings; she may continue to have a parental attitude toward them throughout life. The emotions often condition her ways of thinking, and personal security will be an issue in the way she communicates.

Leo as an urge to state one's opinions very strongly. There is often very little room for compromise when the Lion is on this cusp. This is especially the case if the Sun (Leo's ruling planet) or Mercury are in Capricorn or in a fixed sign.[5] Often there is considerable mental creativity. These people like communicating with children and young people. They often see education as a pleasure, especially when they are allowed to pursue those areas of interest that have a distinctly personal appeal.

Virgo as an orientation to practical issues. This is an individual who has the tendency to see what has to be repaired, healed, or improved in the immediate environment. As this is an earthy sign, there is a very practical approach to relating and communicating. Situations have to be taken care of, tasks have to be completed, and things have to be done. Virgo on this cusp usually strives to find the best and most efficient ways to accomplish all of this. As a child, this person may have made sure that his or her siblings were properly supervised, dressed, fed, and looked after.

Libra as the need to bring peace, harmony, and beauty into the immediate environment. This was the brother or sister who worked to bring resolution to family conflicts, especially conflicts between siblings. The arts and humanities were the favorite subjects at school, and this person tended to complete assignments. Relationships made before the age of twenty-one often lasted into adulthood. Travel is looked upon as a pleasure and this person may easily enjoy arranging and organizing trips for others.

---

5 Taurus, Leo, Scorpio, Aquarius.

Scorpio as an urge to penetrate behind the scenes. The frame of mind is often very perceptive and these people gravitate toward those studies which unlock life's mysteries—science, psychology, or medicine, for example. They desire to unlock life's wealth, so that investment banking and other financial subjects are of great interest. They often had a sibling who was a loner and kept to him or herself. Travel is usually not a favorite pastime, unless there is some practical reason for the journey.

Sagittarius as an avid curiosity about life and a great urge to explore. This sign/cusp placement often produces very good students; love of knowledge (literally, "philosophy") is an important component of their nature. Travel is frequent, and looked forward to with great enthusiasm. Although there tend to be few siblings, the brother or sister can be a great pal, a friend for life, and even a benefactor. Teaching may be as important as learning, to this individual.

Capricorn as a need to use knowledge as a practical tool for advancement. As the third of the earthy signs,[6] this is also a sign/cusp combination that yields a pragmatic turn of mind. Education has to be useful and helpful to family and career. The early environment may have been challenging, for there were many duties and responsibilities, especially to brothers and sisters. This individual may, in childhood, have taken on a parental role.

---

6 Taurus and Virgo are the others.

Aquarius as a highly individualistic way of expressing one-self. This position indicates a person whose way of communicating can be highly intuitive. This is especially the case if Mercury or Uranus (the ruler of Aquarius) are in either Aries, Sagittarius, or one of the airy signs.[7] This is an individual who needs to be in constant communication with many other people. This sign/cusp combination contributes to having many friends who are close enough to be considered as siblings. Science and technology may be of great interest, as well as causes that seem to advance humanitarian efforts.

Pisces as a tendency to be very idealistic. This is a sign/cusp combination that can be very escapist. This person may use travels and intellectual interests as a way to avoid more practical responsibilities, or to balance the more pragmatic obligations of life. There tends to be a universal outlook, which permits this person to envision many ways to approach challenges and problems. This individual may find that he or she has to be very helpful and responsible to a sibling who is in need of emotional assistance.

Planets in the Third House

The Sun in the Third House indicates an urge for continual opportunities to relate and communicate. There is often a need to define oneself through one's intellectual interests. Frequent travel, the desire for continued education, and one's relationships with close friends and siblings will play major roles in

---

7 Gemini, Libra, and Aquarius.

life. This person will often be found in the role of agent, go-between, and maker of connections between people.

The Moon in the Third House gives the tendency to establish personal security through educational and intellectual interests. The emotional and practical needs of close friends and family members will strongly affect one's decisions and actions. Traveling with other family members, or for domestic reasons, is highly likely. With the Moon in this position, opinions about life are constantly "going through phases."

Mercury in the Third House is a very powerful influence, for it is the "natural ruler" of this domicile. The mind is an intensely active and curious instrument when Mercury is placed in this position. In certain cases, the intellect is too strong, leading to an overly analytical nature and a nervous temperament. There is a great need to know and an urge for continuous education. Travel will play an important part in one's life, and there is also likely to be a sibling with whom the individual is especially close.

Venus in the Third House is usually indicative of pleasant relationships with siblings, one of whom may be involved with the arts. There is a strong need to be an agent of harmony within one's immediate family, and a strong desire for intimate and long-lasting friendships. The mind is often balanced, and the cultivation of knowledge is seen as one of life's pleasures.

Mars in the Third House can often lead to dissension with one's brothers and sisters. At the very least, there is apt to be a good deal of competition. These people have a strong need to promote their personal outlook, their opinions, and their thoughts. This can often result in communication conflicts, if the individual cannot or will not accept other people's opinions. Travels may also be undertaken, for personal advancement, and for individual adventure or achievement.

Jupiter in the Third House gives the tendency to travel far and wide, extending short journeys into much longer ones. There is often a strong, highly positive relationship with a sibling (usually an older one) who can become a great influence in one's life. Knowledge is seen as something to be respected, enjoyed, and cultivated.

Saturn in the Third House may bring about a certain depressive state to the mind; at the very least, it indicates a serious and highly responsible frame of reference. On a more positive note, Saturn in this position can indicate a person who has the ability to engage in intensive study and is very self-disciplined intellectually. There is often a sense of responsibility regarding one's siblings. This sometimes indicates that an older brother or sister acted as a parent to this person during childhood.

Uranus in the Third House can be an exceptionally good placement, for it adds intuition and tremendous curiosity about life. It may also lead to unconventional attitudes and opinions that can alienate the individual, marking him or her as an eccentric or some kind of rebel. This in itself does not indicate that the person is antisocial or prone to misbehavior.

It does show, however, a childhood environment in which the individual stood out very clearly on his own.

Neptune in the Third House definitely heightens one's imagination. One can tend to be very creative in writing, especially where fiction and poetry is concerned. On the other hand, this position may lead to excessive daydreaming and inhibit a more rational approach to life. This is an excellent position for filmmakers, screenwriters, and artists of all kinds.

Pluto in the Third House indicates a profound mind and an ever-probing mental attitude. There is the constant urge to develop one's thinking. This is accomplished through the periodic destruction of thoughts and opinions (one's own and others) so that the opportunity for a complete intellectual renewal may take place. This puts a great deal of pressure on the mind: Although this position can indicate an incredibly perceptive person, it also can lead to depression and a certain degree of morbidity.

Third House People, Places, and Things

A. *Astrological Factors*
Quality: Cadent
Quadrant: Northeast
Natural Sign Ruler: Gemini
Natural Planetary Ruler: Mercury

B. *People*

Brothers and sisters in general (especially the eldest)

Close and intimate friends

Neighbors (especially while growing up)

Agents in general, especially travel agents

Bus and taxi drivers

Writers, journalists, lecturers, teachers (through secondary school)

Messengers and delivery people

C. Places and Things

Personal ideas, thoughts, and opinions

The development of mind and one's mental attitudes

Early education and childhood environment

Short distance travel, commuting

Writing, speaking, language skills

General communicative abilities

Books (especially dictionaries) and book shops

Newspapers and magazines

THE FOURTH HOUSE

I Am My Family

The cusp of the Fourth House is called the IC or Immum Coeli, Latin for "at the lowest point in the heavens." Sometimes referred to as the "nadir," this house points to the most subjective part of our lives. This is the portion of the horoscope that deals with our psychological foundations. It is the natural house of the sign Cancer and its ruler, the Moon. As such, the Fourth describes a great deal about our instinctive patterns of behavior. It tells us much about what we have inherited from our family, race, tribe, and nation, as behavioral patterns passed down from generation to generation. In a very distinct sense, we can say that the Fourth House tells us much about our roots. It therefore speaks to us about the familial soil in which we were planted as infants.

The Fourth House is traditionally associated with our mother and our domestic situation in general. It indicates much about the emotional climate surrounding our birth, our mother's life at the time, and the first seven years of life.

This house, considered along with the First and Third Houses, tells the astrologer a great deal about the life circumstances that condition a person's primary and instinctive nature. In essence, this is the most "psychological" of all the houses in the horoscope.

The Fourth House is sometimes more associated with one's father, if the father was the more nurturing, more "maternal" parent. If an individual was raised only by the father, or bonded psychologically to the father especially, or if the sign on the cusp of the Fourth House describes the father rather than the mother, then the Fourth becomes the "father's house." In essence, the Fourth describes our deepest emotional and psychological connection to our family life.

Signs on the Cusp of the Fourth House

A person's relationship to his home life and to that which conditions his sense of personal security is modified in the Fourth House by the sign:

Aries as a need to be in control of one's domestic environment. When Aries rules the fourth, the person is apt to display a distinct sense of territoriality. It is sometimes very difficult to penetrate into the psychological core of this person without meeting some form of resistance. Home, to an individual with this sign/cusp combination, is home base, central headquarters, "the place where I go to anchor my own sense of identity." Aries on this cusp often indicates a very strong mother, one who took the reins of power in the family. This was not a soft and indulgent woman; she was a woman with a very clear sense of who she was, and she had the courage to express it.

Taurus as a need to be surrounded by material comforts and ease. This is an individual who does not like to change her residence very often. Financial security matters a great deal to her, and to her birth family. If Venus, the ruler of Taurus, is well placed in the horoscope, the astrologer knows that the individual never had to want for anything in life. She could rely on her mother, who had considerable common sense, and who was usually quite traditional in her way of raising a family. What was learned in childhood—the values that were inculcated into one's nature—remain a strong presence throughout the life.

Gemini as a need for change and variation. It is highly likely that a person with this sign/cusp combination will have frequent changes of residence. This will be especially the case if Mercury (the ruler of Gemini) is in Gemini or Virgo, Sagittarius, or Pisces. The person does not like the feeling of routine, and can interpret too much stability in his life as "entrapment." There is an inner restlessness and a deep urge to uncover an understanding of oneself that can only be accomplished through a wide variety of experiences. It is likely that one's mother was a very busy person, a woman who had interests other than her children.

Cancer as a profound need for the creation of a stable home foundation. This is the most natural sign for this cusp. The home, one's family life, and especially the relationship one had to one's mother in childhood, are of utmost importance. This is a very "marriage-minded" individual, one who seeks a sense of family nourishment and protection. The astrologer has to examine carefully the position of the Moon, ruler of Cancer, to see the degree to which this may be accomplished. The mother tended to be a very strong presence in the house and this primary relationship can dominate one's life long after one has left home.

Leo as a sense of pride in one's family. In no other sign/cusp combination is the saying, "A man's home is his castle," more true. When the Lion occupies the Fourth House, no matter what the economic circumstances, this position describes an individual with a sense of inner grandeur (or, at the very least, one who aspires to it). The home has to be a place of beauty, but often has more style than substance. There is a great need to be able to stand firm in oneself. If the psychological matrix surrounding the individual in the early life was weak and the mother non-supportive, there will be a lifelong tendency toward self-doubt. The mother held a commanding presence in the life: She was a woman who ruled, and who infused her influence and authority firmly into the individual's inner core.

Virgo as a need to bring healing, wholeness, and refinement into one's domestic life. The sign/cusp placement describes a person who has a deep urge to fix things. This can lead to a life of helpful service, or a very meddlesome and critical busybody. If the individual's psychological matrix is whole and integrated, this is a person who can be counted upon in time of troubles. Virgo on this cusp can give a mixture of common sense and achieved wisdom. When, however, the nature is splintered and overly compartmentalized, Virgo here indicates a person who goes through life with many loose ends and disconnected pieces. The mother reflects this dual possibility: She was either a very efficient person or a woman who never seemed to get her life together.[8]

Libra as a need to bring balance and harmony into all domestic relationships. This sign/cusp combination gives a real need for a peaceful home life. Libra here indicates a person whose home is his sanctuary. It is a place that he inhabits not only for the necessities of daily life, but also as a refuge from the chaos of the world. There is a very strong tendency to share one's life, as this is the sign of marriage and falls on the cusp of the house of family. Yet in no other sign/cusp combination will discord in the home be so psychologically disruptive. The individual has to achieve peace at all costs and, if not careful, can compromise himself. The mother here tends to be an harmonious influence, and more likely than not, a physically attractive person.

Scorpio as an intense need to transform one's initial psychological patterning. This is usually a very challenging placement in the horoscope. Crises in life develop as a result of

---

8 As in the case of all the sign/house combinations, study the positions of the planetary ruler of the sign on the house cusp, and the "natural" planetary ruler of the house. This information, under the heading "People, Places, and Things," is at the end of each of the twelve sections. The Reference Guide will also point to other sources that can widen the reader's knowledge of astrology.

resistance to changing one's instinctual behavior patterns. It thus becomes very essential in this case to create a distinct awareness of the nature of one's psychological foundations. The individual has to emerge from the unconscious waters of her inherited roots and move into the light of self-knowing. This does not mean that she is necessarily the victim of bad parenting or poor maternal influences. It does mean, however, that this person has to "re-root" her connection to her family tree and start a new branch of her own.

Sagittarius as a need to be free from the traditional belief patterns of one's family. This position often indicates a person who leaves home at the earliest age possible. There is a definite sense of independence, along with the attitude that "the world is my home." This sign/cusp combination can easily point to an individual who changes his or her residence regularly, and/or who will reside in another country at some point in life. The family background is usually connected to one of the established religions, to which the individual usually has difficulty adhering. The inner urge is to establish one's own code of ethics and one's own philosophical foundations.

Capricorn as a strong sense of inherited patterns of behavior. This may give rise to a person who builds his life upon established family traditions, or it may indicate a person so circumscribed by the past that he has an inner sense that personal choice and freedom has been curtailed. Capricorn on the Fourth House cusp is commonly experienced as a deep sense of duty and responsibility. This position frequently indicates an individual who finds security in predictability.

This is a person who has a sense of established order within himself, and who feels most comfortable and at ease when expressing himself through his habitual patterns. As a child, he was expected to be mature, and perhaps to fulfill a parental role. Capricorn in this position can indicate the absence of a parent, or, at the very least, the presence of an emotionally cold or reserved parent.

Aquarius as a distinct urge to break away from established patterns of behavior. This is a person who is going to be quite different from his family: He will often stand out, either as the "black sheep," or as the family eccentric. In other instances, this position points to an individual who may be quite the conformist, but who comes from a family of eccentrics! As with everything in natal astrology, many factors in the birth chart have to be considered before the astrologer can draw absolute conclusions. In all cases, however, Aquarius on this cusp will draw upon his own belief system as a source of inner strength and purpose. This is someone who is very fixed— and sometimes *fixated*—in his positions, and who will not easily veer off his own particular course in life.

Pisces as a sense of connection to a universal home. Such a sentiment can give rise to a wanderer, a person who is never content to remain rooted in any one place. There is almost a sense of confinement attached to being too attached! This sign/cusp combination may easily point to a very spiritual and inclusive person, one who feels much more like a child of humanity than the child of a particular set of parents. If Neptune (ruler of Pisces) and/or the Moon are poorly placed in the chart, this position can indicate a home with a history of abuse of alcohol or other drugs. There can be an unsettled feeling, an insecurity which comes from absent, or even harmful, parents.

Planets in the Fourth House

The Sun in the Fourth House points to a need to establish a firm home base as an anchor to personal identity. There is a need to build a strong home life, a foundation and stable psychological anchor. If the early environment was unstable or unbalanced, it will deeply affect the individual's sense of creative potency. People with the Sun in the Fourth have been deeply affected by their family background and often end their lives very close to the physical location where they were raised as children.

The Moon in the Fourth House indicates a person with strong feelings and sentiments. Here, these powerful emotions are usually strongly connected to one's own needs and particular orientation to life. When outside of familiar circumstances, a person with the Moon in the Fourth may not feel particularly safe or comfortable. This person is, however, very nurturing, when in her own environment. A person with the Moon in the Fourth is definitely not one who feels that "everywhere she hangs her hat is home." She tends, however, to be very happy when others feel comfortable in "hanging their hats" in her closet and staying for dinner.

Mercury in the Fourth House indicates a tendency to be very subjective in one's thoughts. This person thinks a great deal about his personal and domestic life. Much energy goes into creating the sense of a secure world, because he feels a need to adapt himself to the ever-changing demands of the "outside" world. If Mercury is in Gemini, Sagittarius, Virgo, or Pisces, in this house, there is a tendency to frequent changes of residence.

Venus in the Fourth House gives a very strong inner need to express oneself harmoniously and artistically. The home is often one's "canvas," and the individual will always create a pleasant and beautiful living space. There is a distinct liking for entertaining in the home and a deep appreciation of the arts in all forms. People with Venus in this house are deeply reluctant to create social disharmony and will work hard to fix any perceived conflict between themselves and others.

Mars in the Fourth House reveals a constant undertone of irritability, restlessness, and high-strung emotions. There is a need to dominate any domestic situation, and an exaggerated tendency to take offense or to feel slighted. If well placed, the individual holds within himself a wealth of inner potency and a reservoir of strength. If Mars is poorly placed in this domicile, it may indicate that the person comes from a childhood in which there was some measure of violence in the home—violence which the individual may continue to find (or create) in adulthood.

Jupiter in the Fourth House underscores a tendency to be accepting of other people and to welcome them into one's "inner sanctum" for advice or protection. This sanctuary can take the form of one's home and/or the comfort of one's inner strength and wisdom. Jupiter in this position often indicates that a person comes from a wealthy or socially established family. Even if this is not the case, the person feels that he or she possesses an internal wealth—often spiritual in nature—that cannot be measured in financial terms.

Saturn in the Fourth House indicates that a person comes from a traditional background, or from one in which personal liberty was somewhat suppressed. If Saturn is well placed, it points to a family life in which duty and responsibility dominated, adding honesty and forthright behavior to one's nature. Depending on other astrological factors that round out the picture, Saturn in the Fourth House can point either to a very strict parent (or stepparent), or to the absence of the father in early childhood. Sometimes it tells the astrologer that the individual was raised by the grandparents.

Uranus in the Fourth House can point to drastic or sudden changes in one's domestic life. It can also indicate an individual who is at odds with his or her background, and is therefore the "oddball" of the family. In any event, this position does not lend itself to the establishment of a life with "a spouse, two kids, and two cars in the garage of a three bedroom house." The individual tends to be socially experimentative by nature, rebelling against all manner of routine behavior.

Neptune in the Fourth House yields a highly impressionable nature and a very sensitive psyche. It often indicates a liking for living by the sea or by water in general. Neptune in this domicile also increases one's urge for artistic self-expression. It stimulates the fantasy life and greatly heightens the imagination. Neptune here may make it difficult for a person to "settle down"; indeed, it often has exactly the opposite effect. In such case, a person may spend a life in search of a reality that may be impossible to find in the practical world.

Pluto in the Fourth House indicates the urge to transform the attachment to one's family background and biological roots. Certain psychological patterns of behavior, often inherited from one's mother, need to be overcome. The individual will spend a great deal of time and effort in the pursuit of a more individualized sense of self. This is a powerful position to stimulate psychological growth. If Pluto is poorly placed in the Fourth, it can lead to rootlessness, constant changes of residence under difficult conditions, and a certain tendency to self-destructive behavior.

Fourth House People, Places, and Things

A. Astrological Factors
Quality: Angular
Quadrant: Northwest
Natural Sign Ruler: Cancer
Natural Planetary Ruler: Moon

B. People
Mother (or most nurturing parent)
Stepmother, grandparents
Ancestors

C. Places and Things

Family background in general, parental influence in particular

Sense of inner security and psychological foundations

Physical home and domestic issues

Office, studio, place of employment

Circumstances surrounding the ending of one's life

Results of one's undertakings

Hotels, motels, and inns

Income from communicative talents, such as writing or speaking

Household fixtures

THE FIFTH HOUSE

I AM MY CREATIVITY

Once we have integrated our sense of personal identity through the activities of the Fourth House, we work to establish our individuality even further through the expansive, fiery nature of the Fifth. It is here that the fruits of the family are produced through the birth of our children. It is also here that the results of our hard work at integrating the various aspects of our personality manifest, as the various forms of our self-expression. The Fifth is most concerned with the outward demonstration of our talents and abilities—it is the house of "show and tell." Here, I make an unmistakable statement of my own identity: Through the Fifth House, I sew my monogram on my shirt and wear it proudly for all to see! If the Second House speaks to us of the money we have in the bank, the Fifth House tells us how we spend it. If the Second House reveals to us our innate, creative possibilities, the Fifth House indicates how we express them.

The Fifth is sometimes called the "party house," as it is associated with our pleasures and pastimes, the games we like to play, and our speculative orientation. People who tend to gamble with love and/or money are very likely to have a strong Fifth House in their natal horoscope. In the Fifth, we can locate our hobbies, vacations, and, most importantly, our natural tendency toward romance. Romance is that feeling which makes us feel special, different, unique, and desired. The Fifth is much more the house of lovers than of marriage partners—who, as we shall soon discover, are found in the Seventh.

Signs on the Cusp of the Fifth House

An individual's urges towards self-expression and the pursuit of personal pleasures are modified in the Fifth House by the sign:

Aries as a tendency to be bold, direct, and projective. The Ram on the cusp of the Fifth is not subtle about who or what he is. Aries in this position says: "I create myself and project myself forward, for all to see and appreciate." People with this sign/cusp combination tend to be a very lusty lovers, unafraid of speculation and adventure, and highly personal in the forms of their creative self-expression. These people usually want to have children, who are often looked upon as an extension of oneself. The Aries/Fifth House cusp parent promotes the advancement of his or her offspring, and is eager about their own advancement in life.

Taurus as a tendency to be intimately concerned with the physical forms of one's creative self-expression. Art and beauty are usually very important facets of the creative self-expression of people born with this sign/cusp placement. They may also be involved with creative financing, so that the use of money becomes an important feature of their life. These people tend to be deeply conservative financially (and romantically): They avoid speculation and gambling, although there may easily be investments in the arts. The attitude towards their children tends to be possessive and cautious.

Gemini as a tendency to have many hobbies, pleasures, and interests. There is also the need to play at romance and love. One may have several lovers at the same time or, at the very least, a number of romantic flirtations during the course of one's life. A person with Gemini on this cusp loves to play games, usually has a positive affinity with children, and tends toward having several children of his own. Writing and other forms of communication are the natural, creative outlets, as are travel and intellectual pursuits of all sorts.

Cancer as a tendency to enjoy pleasures at home. Family and children are very important and the individual's creativity is very much geared to family life. This is not necessarily limited to one's own family—a person can be a writer of children's books, or have cooking as a hobby. Their relationship to children tends to be caring and nurturing, although there can be an overly fearful preoccupation with their safety. Much here, as in all definitions of house/cusp meanings, depends on the nature of the ruling planet of the sign in question. There is a definite avoidance of speculation, for this person would tend to be very security oriented.

Leo as a tendency for a highly personalized form of creativity. As the most natural sign for this cusp, Leo on the Fifth gives a very powerful need to be seen and appreciated as an individual. Unless the Sun, the ruling planet of this sign, is poorly placed, there is an abundance of creative potential, along with the willpower to back it up. Romance plays a very important part in the individual's life, as does the pursuit of sensual pleasure. One's children are well-loved and cared for, although there is a tendency to be a bit dictatorial in directing the course of their lives.

Virgo as a tendency for highly specialized forms of creativity. The forms for the expression of one's talents and abilities are cultivated over a long period of time. Hobbies do form an important part of one's life, and the hands work in tandem with the head to produce lovely objects. A practical approach dominates the urge for pleasure: Gambling and speculation are definitely not favorites on this person's list. Romantic objectives are usually clear and uncomplicated, for there is an avoidance of becoming "lost in love." Children are seen as a natural product of love. As a parent or teacher, however, the individual may be rather fussy about the details of how to raise children properly.

Libra as a tendency to be very artistic and creatively productive. Venus dominates the Fifth House when the Scales are on the cusp, pointing to a definite interest in everything of beauty. There is also the distinct tendency to be heavily romantically involved and to seek out all the possible pleasures which personal love can bring into one's life. This is one area where balance and discrimination are crucial to maintaining personal harmony. Children are usually wanted, and are lovingly accepted. There is a natural orientation to be fair with one's children and not to play favorites.

Scorpio as a tendency to an intense attitude towards romance. This sign/cusp combination is strongly sensual and highly emotionally oriented in terms of its attitude toward personal love. Jealousy and possessiveness toward one's lovers and children can predominate, unless modified by other planetary positions. There are apt to be major turning points in one's creative life. What for years has been a major outlet for the expression of one's interests can seem to shift suddenly, and a door closes shut, never to reopen. Then, after a certain period of time, another door opens, revealing new creative opportunities. This same process can also apply to lovers.

Sagittarius as a tendency to be intensely active creatively. The natural urge is to be creatively expansive and eager to test one's talents and abilities. Life is seen as an adventure, and speculation in love and money is a vital part of what makes life exciting. This sign/cusp combination is therefore strongly geared toward the pursuit of pleasure, seeking all manner of opportunity for its exploration. One of the greatest pleasures and pastimes for Sagittarius on the Fifth is the accumulation of knowledge. This is often accomplished firsthand, through travel and highly personalized educational choices. The attitude toward children is to foster their independence and their own urge to be adventurous in life.

Capricorn as a tendency to be very conservative. Speculation and gambling (indeed, games in general) are not usually cultivated; pleasures and investments tend to be much more safe and long-term in nature. There are, as a rule, few children. Often, they come into one's life late, or through other people. It is therefore very common for people with Capricorn on the Fifth to have stepchildren, or to find themselves involved with young people through their choice of career. If Saturn, ruler of this sign, is poorly placed in the chart, there is a distinct tendency to be a domineering parent and to seek to control one's children. Lovers are usually not plentiful, but, when there is a lover (or a child) in one's life, that individual is usually treated responsibly and with respect.

Aquarius as a tendency to be very experimental in one's creativity. The natural outlets for self-expression with this sign/cusp combination are in the sciences, computers, and the Internet. The urge is to reach as many people as possible as quickly as possible so that continuous interpersonal communication is achieved. This is not the most romantic sign to have on the Fifth: The orientation is much more toward friendship than for unending, intense passion. Individuals with this placement tend to befriend their children and often seek innovative ways of educating them.

Pisces as a tendency to be very artistically and romantically oriented. Film, photography, music, and dance are of special interest to this sign/cusp combination. This is a highly idealistic position when it comes to love and romance. The individual with this position may be all too easily swept away by personal love. Self-compromise often accompanies the pursuit of sensual pleasure when Pisces is on this cusp. The romantic life is usually filled with complications. Although there can be great joys and enormous highs in this area of life, equally great disappointments may also result. Depending on the positions of Neptune and Jupiter, the two rulers of the Fish, children can be a source of great personal upliftment, or can become a great burden.

Planets in the Fifth House

The Sun in the Fifth House is an indication of a person's continuous need for self-expression. The urge to be actively creative and demonstrate one's talents and abilities is a vital factor in life. This position also gives a great desire for romance, the appreciation for a good time, and the enjoyment of life's pleasures.

The Moon in the Fifth House intensifies the emotional nature where one's attachment to children and lovers are concerned. There is a need for intimacy in all personal relationships and a love of shared emotional experiences. This is the area in life that is most likely to "go through phases," with very changeable circumstances affecting one's creative and romantic avenues of self-expression.

Mercury in the Fifth House gives the need to express one's thoughts and opinions creatively. Writing, speaking, and traveling may, accordingly, become essential outlets in this person's life. There is often a child with whom one becomes especially close, or a younger sibling who occupies the role of one's child.

Venus in the Fifth House greatly highlights the artistic and romantic associations of this house. It is usually easy to attract romantic involvements, and there is a notable love of life's pleasures. If Venus is supported by her sign placement and by her relationship to the other planets, a child is quite often the source of a great blessing, and one's relationships with young people in general tend to be very positive.

Mars in the Fifth House reveals a strong sensual nature that, if not tempered or modified with love and grace, can lead to enormous difficulties. Strife and break-ups, in one's relationships with lovers and children, are likely unless Mars is otherwise well positioned in the horoscope. If well positioned, Mars here strongly indicates that there will be cohesive direction in the expression of one's creative and romantic urges and drives.

Jupiter in the Fifth House gives a person a love of adventure, sports, and speculation. These are individuals who are convinced of their "luck," and for whom taking chances is a normal part of life. There is often a great deal of joy in relationship to children, and a rewarding romantic life. This position definitely contributes to an optimistic outlook, but, should Jupiter not be supported by sign or the other planets, life may be seen through rose-tinted glasses, resulting in self-deception and excessive idealism.

Saturn in the Fifth House is indicative of a person who is often responsible for other people's children. The individual may be cast in the role of stepparent, foster parent, teacher, or guardian. The relationship with one's own child, especially the eldest, may be burdensome. In terms of one's romantic life, certain limitations or restrictions are likely. Frequently Saturn in the Fifth points to a tendency for older lovers.

Uranus in the Fifth House as the tendency towards unconventional behavior in one's love life. This can indicate relationships that appear highly unusual from the perspective of the prevailing norms of society. Uranus in this position may also indicate that one has a child who is very different from others. Depending on other factors in the chart, such a child may be a gifted genius or an antisocial rebel.

Neptune in the Fifth House can bring about a great deal of self-deception in one's romantic involvements. If Neptune is poorly placed, there is a tendency to become intimately involved with people who are emotionally unstable and unreliable. Neptune here can lead to severe losses from gambling or other forms of addictive pleasures and may point to having a child or children who suffer from these tendencies. The more positive indications of Neptune in the Fifth lead to highly creative interests in the arts, a deep pleasure in spiritual pursuits, and a gift for working with people in need of comfort and support.

Pluto in the Fifth House is an excellent placement for working with children who need to have their life direction transformed. A well positioned Pluto here leads to a never-ending supply of creative energy. Romantic involvements are usually not particularly numerous, but they are intense and have profound meaning and consequences for the people involved.

When Pluto is in this house, many of the deepest lessons to be learned in life come through one's love affairs.

Fifth House People, Places, and Things

Astrological Factors
    Quality: Fixed
    Quadrant: Northwest
    Natural Sign Ruler: Leo
    Natural Planetary Ruler: The Sun

People
    Children (especially the first born)
    Actors, actresses, and entertainers
    Second sibling
    Friends of one's spouse or business partner
    Lovers and romantic interests

Places and Things
    Personal creative self-expression
    Courtship and romance
    The pleasures of life
    Vacations
    Hobbies, sports, speculation
    Adornments and jewelry
    Clothing and costumes
    Theater, circuses, and sports arenas
    Gambling casinos
    Raffles and lotteries
    Family wealth

The Sixth House

I Am My Health and Work

One of the names astrologers like to give to this area of the horoscope is "the house of self-improvement." The Sixth House reveals those tools, methods, techniques, and processes we use in order to perfect that sense of ourselves which is projected through the Ascendant. It is also the domicile that brings greater definition to the creative activities of self-expression found in the Fifth. It is through the activities of the Sixth that a person particularizes and further individualizes him or herself. This process requires a great deal of elimination of what is outworn, outmoded, and outdated in ourselves, so that our "self-becoming" is consistent and productive. In this respect, the Sixth is very revealing of our health, for elimination is an aspect of both our physical and psychological well-being. In addition to showing what we must eliminate, the Sixth also reveals what we must add in order to amplify our creativity and improve ourselves. All told, the Sixth points us in the direction of perfecting our basic orientation to life, and to those processes that serve to bring greater and more precise definition to our individuality.

The Fifth House is by nature expansive: It amplifies what we structured, in the Fourth, as our basic psychological foundation. The Fifth proclaims with a trumpet call: "This is what I can create!" "OK, fine," say the experiences of the Sixth, "but how can you perfect that creativity, that projective sense of yourself, so that it fits into a larger social picture? Remember, we are about to enter the more collective, *southern hemisphere* of your chart. Have you perfected yourself enough, so that you are ready to withstand the scrutiny of society? Have you gathered unto yourself enough practical tools and techniques to make a contribution to the world?"

We could say that the Sixth House tells us much about how we use our time, energy, and talents in our everyday life. It reveals much about how we face the challenges of the "workaday" world and how we approach the more routine aspects of our lives. It shows who and what helps us, and who and what may hinder us from achieving our physical and emotional perfection.

Employees, co-workers (especially those in lesser positions), domestic helpers, and pets are therefore all inhabitants of this house.

Signs on the Cusp of the Sixth House

A person's general health, attitudes and aptitudes in terms of work, and relationships to helpers are modified in the Sixth House by the sign:

Aries as the urge to prove oneself. This sign/house combination produces an orientation to life which states: "I am my work!" There is a strong urge to attack and conquer any and all obstacles that may come up on the job. This is either a person who feels totally competent at every phase of every task, or one who has to prove his dominance, to himself and to others. In either case, there is a tendency to see that whatever one does as a reflection of personal competency. Problems come up with others when Aries on this cusp seeks to direct and control, without taking other people's feelings or capabilities into consideration. Pet owners with this sign on the Sixth definitely see their animals as intimate extensions of themselves. Health issues would concern the head, face, and especially the nose and eyes.

Taurus with a highly practical approach to these matters. The health is often robust and the constitution strong, when the Bull is on the Sixth. As the thyroid gland and metabolism are sensitive areas of the body, difficulties with this house can lead to sluggishness, laziness, and resistance to one's job. If however, these parts of the physical system are working well, the individual has a never-ending supply of energy to accomplish whatever needs to be done. Jobs and tasks may still be approached with a certain circumspection and caution, but the final result will not only be solid and correct, but will also be as physically beautiful as the situation permits. There is generally a caring but possessive attitude toward pets, who may easily be overfed! Co-workers and employees are treated kindly, but will be expected to earn their salary.

Gemini with an ability to tackle many situations simultaneously. The variety and versatility inherent in the Twins comes out in the work sphere through a generally agile and adjustable nature. There is a liking for those activities that permit a person to vary his or her routine, for boredom can easily accompany a job that is too repetitive. Skill is required, to know when to make a move that will enhance one's career, rather than change jobs merely for the sake of change itself. These are people whose communication skills will be tested; travel may also play an important part in their professional life. Health issues involve the nervous system, and anxiety can arise through an overly analytical mental nature. Smoking should be avoided, as the lungs are apt to be quite sensitive. There is a tendency to have more than one pet, with whom one develops a fairly close relationship.

Cancer as the need to nourish and to be nourished. This is an ideal sign for being in a position in which one has to be sensitive to people's emotional needs. A psychological counselor, doctor or medical technician, food service worker, or real estate consultant all fit very naturally into this sign/ house combination. Problems can come up when the individual takes her job, or problems in the work environment, too personally. Health is focused on digestion, which is often related to one's emotional well-being. Domestic pets play an important part in one's life. There is the definite orientation to make one's cat or dog a real member of the family or, when exaggerated, into one's child.

Leo with strength and pride. If the Sun, ruler of this sign, is well placed in the horoscope, the health is very good and there is an abundance of vitality and creative energy. A great deal of attention goes into one's work, because success on the job is very important. These people like to have a leading position at their place of employment. They should, however, make sure that they actually earn the respect of their co-workers or employees, rather than demand it. Natural areas of employment will be in the theater, arts, and entertainment industries, and in work that involves children. Professions that deal with clothing, jewelry, and other forms of adornment are also natural to this sign/cusp combination. Pets can be a source of pride and are usually well-groomed and nourished—cats, of course, will be a natural favorite of the Lion on this cusp.

Virgo with care and precision. As this is the natural sign ruler of this house, Virgo on this cusp indicates a person who pays a great deal of attention to personal health, work, and all other areas naturally associated with this house. There is the tendency to be very fastidious at whatever job the individual undertakes. An urge for perfection in all and everything is very pronounced, and lessons in discrimination and prioritization are often important aspects of this individual's life experience. This position can indicate a person who is just too fussy about details, and is overly critical about what she does and who she does it with. Yet such perfectionism, when balanced and well integrated, can make for an amazingly accomplished individual—one who excels at everything he or she sets out to do. Health involves the intestines and, accordingly, the correct absorption of the nutrients found in one's diet. As a rule, there is a liking for keeping the body fit, although there may be an undue emphasis upon one's physical appearance and condition. Pets usually play an important part in one's life.

Libra with balance. Relationships in the workplace are very important to a person with this sign/cusp combination. There is a need for fairness and justice, in the assignment of work and the completion of tasks. This is a person who has a need for beauty in their working environment and who would tend to decorate his or her office accordingly. Jobs that involve dealing with the public, management-worker relationships, general consulting, the arts, and fashion are very natural to a person whose Sixth House is ruled by a sign of Venus. Pets are well looked after but are seen as an integrated part of one's life. They are not usually given exaggerated importance relative to the rest of one's concerns and relationships. Health is often strongly affected by the condition of one's relationships—an imbalance in one's personal life may result in a weakening of one's physical condition. The parts of the body that are the most sensitive when Libra rules the Sixth are the diaphragm, urinary tract, and the kidneys.

Scorpio with intensity. Wherever Scorpio appears in a chart, there is the urge to create transformation. This sign/cusp combination can indicate a person who secretly seeks to dominate in the workplace for the purpose of personal advancement. Yet it may also indicate an individual who functions to bring order out of chaos, harmony through the conflicts found in the workplace, and new strength where there was once weakness. So much depends on the general ego structure of the individual in question, when determining Scorpio's direction and influence on any of the cusps of the chart! As this is the sign of regeneration, Scorpio on the Sixth has the tendency to allow the individual great sustaining and recuperative powers. Good health, for these people, is very much a question of the emotions, because this is the sign of our sexual and desire natures. As with everything else that is scorpionic, there will either be a tremendous attraction or a strict avoidance (and even fear) of pets and animals.

Sagittarius with enthusiasm. An exuberant sign, Sagittarius brings hopefulness and optimism into the workplace. This is a person who tends to add vision to any task; as a result, he or she may exaggerate their place in the larger scheme of things, or may bring in just the right amount of understanding to improve output. As a rule, this sign/cusp combination brings advancement in one's job and good relationships between oneself and one's co-workers or employees. Jobs most often associated with this position have to do with sports and recreation, the travel and hotel industry, teaching, and publishing. Health is often robust, for a positive attitude to one's physical condition is typical. Areas of greatest sensitivity are the liver, hips, and thighs. Pets are usually large, often numerous, and sometimes exotic. Great Danes, iguanas, big tomcats, and (of course) a love of horses, are typical examples of the Centaur on the Sixth House cusp.

Capricorn with care and concern for success. This is a very practical sign/house combination resulting in a person's profound interest in making the most out of any work situation. The urge for advancement is very strong, as is the ability to be highly efficient and organized. An individual with Capricorn on the cusp of the Sixth takes her job seriously and does not mind putting in those extra hours in order to fulfill her tasks. The means justifies the end to Capricorn on the Sixth. Relationships with co-workers and employees can be strained if the person is too demanding or controlling. If Saturn, ruler of this sign, is not well placed in the horoscope, the individual tends to feel held back, restricted, and dissatisfied in job-related situations. Health can be an issue if there is too much general pessimism about life. The areas of greatest sensitivity are the bones and joints (especially the knees), spine, and lower back. Pets are usually quite important, and there is a tendency to be very responsible and caring of them.

Aquarius with a certain degree of unconventionality. If there are any health-related problems, this individual is likely to explore alternative methods of healing. There is an interest in the relationship between the mind and the body and a tendency to seek out "New Age" techniques of personal development. As this is the sign furthest from Leo (which is ruled by the Sun), health problems can relate to circulation, and there may be a consequent lack of vitality. Since these people believe in "mind over matter," they are likely, however, to rebalance their life energies by cultivating a right mental attitude. Work is an area in which communications and right human relationships will be predominant issues. Those areas that are humanitarian in nature, or computer-related, will figure prominently in the lives of people with the Water Bearer on the cusp. Pets that are unusual or exotic are preferred, especially those that are more independent by nature—cats, rather than dogs, for example.

Pisces with a definite emotional overtone. This is a sign/cusp combination that can bring a great deal of compassion into the workplace. It indicates a person who is geared to working with people who are in need of helpful support: It points to professions of a medical, psychological, or spiritual nature. Another facet of Pisces on this cusp adds vision and a love of beauty. This makes such individuals easily attracted to the arts, music, film, and other practical outlets for the creative imagination. Escapism is another aspect of this complex sign. Depending on the rest of the horoscope, this sign placement can point to a person who is never satisfied by any job, and who is always on the move from one work position to another, in search of an elusive perfection. Health is strongly conditioned by one's emotional state, and the body can be very sensitive to all drugs and medications. This person finds her pets in animal shelters, or picks up strays from the streets.

Planets in the Sixth House

The Sun in the Sixth House reveals a general concern for one's place in the scheme of things. "Where do I fit in?" is a frequent question. Work is very much an issue and, depending on the Sun's relationship to the other planets, can be an area of the greatest trial or one of amazing success. There is often a preoccupation with health and the practicalities of life, and a real need to establish oneself in the workaday world.

The Moon in the Sixth House gives the need to help other people through an occupation that involves some form of service to the general public. Matters concerning health and jobs "go through phases" when the Moon is in this position, because one's emotional nature contributes greatly to the success and well-being of these important facets of life.

Mercury in the Sixth House indicates a high degree of adaptability, versatility, and change in terms of one's approach to work. This can mean an incredible restlessness with an inability to remain constant in one's chosen field, or an extraordinary talent for tackling any situation that may come up.

Venus in the Sixth House brings harmony and balance into the workplace. There is a tendency to enjoy positive relationships with one's co-workers and employees, and to have a general sense of fair play. Good general health and a balanced constitution are also gifts of Venus, when she is placed in this position.

Mars in the Sixth House can bring discord and competitiveness into the work environment. The urge is to be dominant in one's job. Unless this is carried out with some degree of diplomacy, the individual can find that other people will work against his or her success. Drive and determination are also indicated, but achievement must be coupled with right human relationships.

Jupiter in the Sixth House adds optimism, vision, and understanding to one's job. There is often a sense of support for others that extends beyond the scope of personal ambition. If afflicted, Jupiter in this position can give a tendency to over-indulgence in food and drink, leading to problems with the liver and general digestion.

Saturn in the Sixth House brings either a strong sense of responsibility, or a feeling of burden attached to one's job. Very often fear of failure is a facet of this position. This fear brings about either a defeatist and pessimistic attitude, or stimulates the individual to work harder. If strongly placed by sign and in relation to the other planets, this position indicates the ability to withstand all types of illness; if poorly placed, there is a tendency toward chronic or inherited illnesses.

Uranus in the Sixth House can give a very erratic and unconventional attitude to work. This may bring about a highly successful, individualistic career; or there may be a constant urge to change jobs frequently, due to a marked dissatisfaction with routine. The health can be suddenly challenged by nerves or unusual factors that are hard to treat. In any event, the individual prefers to seek out healing that is alternative to traditional Western medicine.

Neptune in the Sixth House gives great resourcefulness in the accomplishment of tasks, and the ability to be very helpful to others in need. If poorly placed in this house, there is a tendency toward an impractical attitude in any work situation. The use of alcohol and other drugs should be carefully monitored. All illnesses will have a strong emotional component, so that the individual's psychological nature must be included in any form of health treatment.

Pluto in the Sixth House brings new life into the workplace. Enormous dedication and willpower can be exerted to the accomplishment of all tasks, when Pluto is well placed in this house. If afflicted by the other planets, or if the general ego structure predisposes, this position indicates a person who can abuse her position and seek to dominate other people for her own benefit. Pluto in this position is often a gift to our health, for it indicates profound regenerative and recuperative abilities.

Sixth House People, Places, and Things

Astrological Factors
  Quality: Cadent
  Quadrant: Northwest
  Natural Sign Ruler: Virgo
  Natural Planetary Ruler: Mercury

B. People
  Co-workers
  Employees, servants
  Doctors and nurses
  Maternal aunts and uncles

C. Places and Things
  Work, and attitude to job
  Tools, techniques, methods, and processes of self-improvement
  General health issues
  Pets and small animals
  Medical offices or laboratories
  Children's finances
  Sanitation issues
  Labor issues

The Seventh House

I Am Myself with You

The Sixth was the last of the "personal houses." Its function was to bring a more precise and refined definition to one's sense of self. In effect, the individuality (First House) has been given its resources (Second House), an ability to communicate (Third House), a family and psychological foundation (Fourth House), creative talents (Fifth House), and finally a sense of service, an urge for health and well-being, and a good haircut (Sixth House). The individual is now ready to go out into society and roam the pathways of the "social or collective houses" in the southern hemisphere of the horoscope. But first, he or she must find a mate—a partner, a companion—to share the adventure. This is the function of the Seventh House.

If the First House (especially the Ascendant) speaks primarily about "you," then the Seventh House (especially the Descendant) reveals the "not you." It is through the sign on the Seventh House cusp that the astrologer determines what quality in others attracts you the most. This is, more often than not, a quality in yourself—you either do not see it, and/ or you need to incorporate it into your own personality and character to give you a sense of your own wholeness. The Seventh House is thus the domicile of relationships, specifically of relationships of a very special kind. The First House speaks about the relationship I have with myself, and with myself relative to the world in general. The Fifth House tells me about my relationships with lovers, but the Seventh is much more a house of partnership. It is traditionally the house of marriage, and it is in the Seventh that we set out to find our life partner. Astrology, however, has to adjust to the times in which we live. Very often people are in committed and profound relationships without being married. So, we have to broaden the definition of the Seventh House, and call it the house of "significant others." It is most certainly a place of greater maturity, relationship, than the Fifth. A relationship might start out as a torrid love affair, or an "amazing attraction," in the Fifth. This becomes a Seventh House relationship when the two people commit to each other and, intending to share their lives, do so in an exclusive one-on-one contract.

There are two other important facets to the Seventh House business partnerships and competitors. Venus is the natural ruler of this house, and of its sign, Libra. She is also the natural ruler of the Second House, and of its sign, Taurus. Libra is an airy, communicative, social sign, while Taurus is an earthy, practical, and materially polarized sign. In the Seventh House, Venus brings her more pragmatic interests into the sphere of relationships; hence, the men and women with whom we enter into financial contracts and partnerships are also found in this house.

We often have the most serious battles and conflicts with the people who matter most to us. If we process and understand our relationships correctly, we will see that the faults we find in our partners, and the points of controversy in our relationships, are very often reflections of what we need to heal in ourselves. Thus the Seventh House speaks to us about our "shadow self"—the part of our own nature (First House) that is reflected in the "open warfare" we have with others.

Signs on the Cusp of the Seventh House

The nature of our urge for relationships and close partnerships is modified in the Seventh House by the sign:

Aries as a potent need to find ourselves in others. As Libra is on the Ascendant (when Aries is here), the creation of relationship is very much connected to our self-image. With Aries on the cusp of the Seventh, relationship becomes one's initial orientation to life. Relationships are often made without an awareness of their deeper consequences. The need to be in relationships is so strong that one often forgets that there has to be a greater degree of objectivity in their formation than the individual with Aries on the First House cusp is willing to make. In effect, this sign/cusp combination can make one so obsessed with "the other" that one's own identity becomes lost. There is also the tendency to make the other person into one's perfect ideal of a partner, thereby losing sight of the other person's true nature. If the ego structure is mature,

Aries on this cusp can bring great vitality and direction into any relationship, creating new avenues for the exploration of life.

Taurus as a need for stability, security, and commitment. Libra rules this house, and is a sign of Venus; as Taurus is the other sign of Venus, this is basically a very positive sign/cusp combination. Taurus seeks surety and loyalty. The urge is to create relationship on a firm foundation of practical values. The individual does not want many partners. If other factors support this indication, this is a person who seeks monogamy and long-term commitment. Taurus is a sensual and earthy sign, so the physical beauty of one's partner is a major element of the relationship. As Scorpio is on the Ascendant, the sexual content of relationships will be of great importance. Sometimes the sexual side of a person's urge for partnership can eclipse more important, essential values: Taurus on the Seventh House cusp can mistake the outer form for the inner essence of a person. Money will be another important element in partnerships. This should be no problem if Venus is well placed in the horoscope, but, if the "Love Goddess" (who is also the "Wealth Goddess") is afflicted, money problems will be a source of conflict in most relationships.

Gemini as a need for variety and versatility. This sign/house combination is often an indication of a person who tends to have more than one relationship at a time or who, at the very least, will marry or become seriously committed in partnership on several occasions. This individual requires a partner who is intellectually stimulating, entertaining, and avoids routine. Travel will be an important part of the relationship. As Sagittarius is on the cusp of the Ascendant, the individual has a definite independent streak and will require partners who are self-sufficient and able to spend periods of time comfortably on their own. This sign/cusp combination is certainly not an indication of a need for inseparable togetherness. Relationships prosper with Gemini on this cusp when there is a strong mental base, clear communication, and room for independent activities.

Cancer as a strong tendency for fundamental support. As Capricorn is on the Ascendant, marriage and solid relationships are seen as essential to a stable position in society. The individual is seeking a partner who will provide a firm foundation upon which individual and family growth is possible. The partner should be able to bring comfort, nourishment, and emotional security. This is definitely not a person who is divorce-oriented—once committed, Cancer on the Descendant seeks to stay put. It is very difficult for these people to take on their own emotional responsibilities. Very often they will project their emotional needs upon the partner, essentially demanding that the "significant other" be the vehicle and the cure for all of their own emotional problems and instability. Partnerships in business, and people who can be supportive of one's career, will have great importance.

Leo as the need for loyalty. As Aquarius is on the Ascendant, friendship in relationships is most important. The basis for any real and lasting friendship is consistency and communality of interests. Since Leo is on the cusp of the Seventh, all of the above are essential to a firm and long-term relationship. Leo is one of the fixed signs, which emphasize the urge for permanence. This is a person who takes great pride in choosing a partners, and needs to find in the other person a sense of flair and a certain creative spirit. The partner is looked to as being a sort of hero or heroine, a person who is courageous and brave, stalwart and faithful. At the same time, the partner has to be adoring but not overly possessive. This is because Aquarius on the Ascendant requires a tremendous amount of personal freedom and the loyal Leo on the Descendant is expected to be supportive of this independent type.

Virgo as need for practicality. This sign/cusp combination is looking for a real "help-mate," one who can be down-to-earth for the more ethereal Pisces Ascendant person. A man or woman with Virgo on the Seventh is looking for a partner with very specific qualities. There is the urge to find in the other the perfection that is lacking in oneself. That is a tall order, and a heavy responsibility to place on another person's shoulders. With this sign on the Seventh, relationships are challenged as the ideal comes face-to-face with the real. The Pisces Ascendant runs away from the harsh reality of life— and the partner's all too human personality! This Descendant also gives a person the need to be of service in relationships. This tendency can manifest in two ways. The first way is service through an idealistic urge to cure, heal, or "save" others from themselves. All too often this is a projection of the person's own sense of incompleteness. The second approach is a realistic and sincere orientation to service, adopted by someone who has the practical tools to be successful in this respect.

Libra as a fundamental need to share one's life with another. Since Libra is the natural sign of this house, there is no other sign/cusp combination that is stronger or more suitable for partnership. This potent combination, however, does not necessarily produce the best or most beneficial result. Yes, there is a natural urge to be fair and just in relationship. But as Aries is on the cusp of the First, the urge for self-projection can easily unbalance this potential equanimity. "Be cooperative, do things my way!" may often be the resulting attitude. Libra has to be careful not to overly idealize the partner. There is a tendency to put others up on pedestals, as if to say: "My partner is a true god(dess), so lovely, so perfect. If such a being loves me, then I too, am someone special." If, however, the nature of the personality is more whole and integrated, this sign/cusp combination may indeed lead to great harmony, beauty, and love in personal relationships. Libra is the sign of marriage and people who have the Scales on the Seventh are seeking long-term commitments.

Scorpio as a vehicle for transformation. Relationships do not reflect the romantic idealism of Libra, the unbridled fun and passion of Leo, or the lighthearted joy of Gemini, when Scorpio is on the Seventh House cusp. Partnerships are processes for deep and profound change. Through the effects that the Scorpio Descendant person brings into other people's lives, and through the changes which are invited into the life through one's choice of partners, transmutation happens. Taurus, which is devoutly connected to the status quo, is on the cusp of the Ascendant. Scorpio is the sign of death and rebirth. Scorpio challenges the nature of the stability that

Taurus seeks to create. But such challenges, and the relationships which bring them, can bring about even greater wealth, more refined life values, and increased vitality. The path of relationships may have its conflicts when Scorpio is on the Descendant, but the promise for an ever-growing, ever-evolving partnership is also at its greatest.

Sagittarius as a need for expansive experiences and growth. Relationships create the potential for adventure and partners point the way to new worlds of opportunity. This is the optimistic perspective which is associated with this sign/cusp combination. Gemini is on the Ascendant: The joining of the Twins to the Centaur points the way to a free-spirited, open, and fundamentally friendly attitude to all forms of partnership. Emotional depth, deep passionate attachment, and jealous insecurity are not part of this picture. If it is a torrid, earth-shaking, "I love you forever and ever—it's only you and me in the world" type of relationship one is searching for, then this is definitely not the place for you! Sagittarius on the Seventh expects the partner to be self-sustaining and not to make too many emotional demands. Life is an exciting adventure, filled with travel, philosophical explorations, and uplifting thoughts; relationships are expected to support and supplement these ideals.

Capricorn as a need for structure, order, and form. When Cancer is on the Ascendant, an individual may go through many emotional ups and downs, uncertainties, and insecurities. Capricorn on the Seventh House cusp expresses the need to find firm ground—a stable contact with the earthy element. This fulfillment is sought through relationships.

Capricorn on the Descendant points to cultivating partnerships that build on the foundations of the personality. Thus, one has the sense of being able to stand up in the world, for one has a steel frame and a strong defense. Such an orientation leads to relationships with older and/or established people. One has a liking for those who have achieved standing in the world, or who, by their own inner strength, help one toward the achievement of one's goals. On the other hand, this sign/cusp combination may attract into one's life people who cannot be penetrated, who wear a shield, and who are not emotionally available.

Aquarius as a need for the unusual. When Leo is on the Ascendant, life is very dramatic. With Aquarius on the Seventh House cusp, one is sure of attracting into one's life people who are out of the ordinary and who provide a lot of interesting and surprising circumstances. Leo likes to be the center of attention and Aquarius rules crowds. On a practical level, Aquarius on the Descendant brings the individual into contact with many different people, and with groups and organizations within which Leo can shine. People who are very Aquarian by nature make many social relationships. This sign/cusp combination allows the individual to branch out, extend, and move away a bit from leonine egocentricity. Leo is very personal; Aquarius is the most impersonal of all the signs. There are real benefits to this house cusp for a Leo Ascendant. The "King of the Zodiac" can leave his royal trappings behind and, through his relationships, more easily circulate among all people, making his creative contributions accordingly.

Pisces as a need to widen personal understanding of life. Although this may not be the conscious purpose of many people with the Fish on the Descendant, it is nonetheless the lesson that is learned throughout their relationships. Pisces dissolves—in this case, it dissolves the sense of separation that often accompanies a Virgo Ascendant. While Virgo likes to find a place for everything and have everything in its place, Pisces knows that everything is already where it should be. Relationships may be very challenging to detail-oriented Virgo rising people, as they normally attract others who are described by the most universal and inclusive of all the signs, Pisces. This sign/house combination is also indicative of the urge to help people in distress. This is one of the reasons why people with Virgo on the First House cusp are frequently involved with individuals who are in need of medical, psychological, or pragmatic organizational skills.

Planets in the Seventh House

The Sun in the Seventh House indicates a person who is always involved in forging social ties that serve to define or complement himself. There is a deep dependence on relationships and personal interactions, so that one's own creativity and individuality is in constant response to other people's initiatives.

The Moon in the Seventh House is a position which indicates a person who is very responsive to other people's emotional needs. It is an excellent placement for a consultant or therapist. There is a tendency to early marriage as well as a need for close interdependence with all partners.

Mercury in the Seventh House gives the ability to be extremely sociable and at ease with people in general. There is a natural urge to exchange opinions and a strong drive to communicate and relate. The individual has to take care that his or her opinions are not overly swayed by other people's thought processes.

Venus in the Seventh House is usually a lovely position as it enhances one's social skills and creates many positive opportunities for relationships. There is a definite skill at matching people and coordinating social functions and events.

Mars in the Seventh House is often an indication of conflict. There can be a lot of competition generated with this position, for there is an urge to dominate one's partners. Mars in this house may also speak about a tendency to violent or disruptive relationships.

Jupiter in the Seventh House usually engenders benefits from relationships. The partner may be well traveled, highly educated, and philosophical in nature. The individual with Jupiter in this house is helpful to others and is very well-intentioned where other people are concerned. If Jupiter is not well positioned, either by sign and/or the other planets, the partner can be slothful and highly opinionated.

Saturn in the Seventh House brings a lot of responsibility into relationship. One of the most important life lessons has to do with correct sharing on all levels. Very often the partner is older, but sometimes it is the person with this position who is the figure of authority in the relationship. Marriage may occur late in life; if so (and if the lessons about sharing have been learned), it is usually happier than one's earlier partnerships.

Uranus in the Seventh House brings about sudden changes in relationships, or it causes relationships to begin like a bolt of lightning coming out of the sky. One is usually attracted to highly unusual and individualistic types of people, who are not given over to routine and who may be eccentric and/or erratic in their behavior. Group affiliations and relationships with highly specialized or unusual organizations is also a strong tendency with Uranus in this position.

Neptune in the Seventh House can manifest as an attraction to people who are truly giving and self-sacrificing, or to those who are truly self-destructive. It is difficult for the individual to see her partners clearly, and it is therefore very important to be able to look at others without a veil of illusion. This position also leads one to help others in psychological or spiritual distress.

Pluto in the Seventh House brings about a certain intensity in personal relationships. It is a position that can bring into one's life a partner who functions as a source of renewal and strength both for oneself and others. If poorly placed, Pluto in this house is very detrimental to relationship longevity and can bring about great deceit.

Seventh House People, Places, and Things

A. Astrological Factors
Quality: Angular
Quadrant: Southwest
Natural Sign Ruler: Libra
Natural Planetary Ruler: Venus

People
Husband, wife, partner
Rivals and competitors
Opponents in a law suit
Lawyers and mediators
Consultants in general (including astrologers)
Mother's family (especially the maternal grand-
    mother)
Second child
Thid brother or sister

Places and Things
Marriage and general attitude to partnerships
The hidden side to oneself
What we seek to attract into our lives
Agreements, contracts, pacts, alliances
Fine arts
Places where lovers meet

The Eighth House

I Am Transformed

This is one of the most complex houses of the horoscope. It contains some of the most complicated, important, and challenging issues that we face in life. In this respect, the Eighth is the house of: death, sexuality, and other people's resources. It is also the area of great personal challenges on many levels. No wonder it, and its sign ruler Scorpio, have such a notorious reputation among astrology students!

All of the issues under the banner of the Eighth House have one thing in common—they are all either *transformative* processes or the results of such processes. Although an examination of this house tells much about the nature of an individual's physical death, the Eighth also has a lot to do with our psychological and spiritual death. It is in this portion of the horoscope that we see how we may "die" to one stage of our existence (or to one phase of our emotional development) and then be reborn into our next step in life.

We find our mates in the Seventh House, but it is through our sexual contact with another person (and the emotional dynamics that always follow) that our "urge to merge" is either fulfilled or dissolved. The sexual nature, for the vast majority of human beings, is either a sure path to personal and interpersonal regeneration and growth, or it brings about very deep complications that are quite destructive in their effects. Sometimes, sexuality does both simultaneously. Although it is true that once we become sexual the beauty, purity, and innocence of childhood is lost, at the same time the opportunities to grow and evolve are set in motion. It is equally true that once a relationship becomes sexual, the dynamics between the two people involved are changed forever. There is no going back: The relationship is now on a direct course either for evolution or annihilation. The area of sexuality is very important, and the Eighth House shows us how it is so filled with fears and proscriptions, as well as great joy and release!

When we mate and marry we join our physical, emotional, and spiritual resources with those of the other person. As the Eighth House is *the second from the Seventh,* it involves the resources of our partners, from the standpoints of marriage and of business.[9] In a more general sense, the

9 The second house from the First in the chart has to do with our own resources. This formula can be applied anywhere in the horoscope: the Sixth House (the second house from the Fifth House of our children) speaks about the resources of our offspring, while the Fourth House (the second house from the Third House of our brothers and sisters) tells the astrologer much about the resources of our siblings. These are examples of what we call the "secondary meanings" of the houses and we will dis-

Eighth speaks about money that comes to us from our general dealings with others, and about the rewards that come to us from our creative self-expression.[10] It is also the house of divorce settlements, wills, and legacies as well as the house of royalties, stock dividends, and money which is won or lost coming from any investments we may have made.

Finally, the Eighth is the house of death. There is an ancient spiritual saying that reminds us: "Death is but a change of form; life is immortal." The house opposite the Eighth is the Second, the house which contains all of our material resources, possessions, and, most importantly, our attitude toward money, having, and owning. This is the domicile of Taurus, symbolized by the "Golden Calf" in the Old Testament. Taurus is the ruler of all the forms of the earth. Scorpio and the Eighth House speak about the death and destruction of form on the one hand; on the other, they speak about the regeneration of form the new possibilities that life offers us, so we may enrich ourselves on many levels. The price that we usually have to pay for this renewal is death, release, and detachment.

---

cuss this facet of astrology in the last section, "The Secondary Meanings of the Houses."

10 Another meaning of the Fourth house has to do with "endings," or the results of our activities. The Eighth House is the fourth from the Fifth and thus speaks about the results (and especially the financial results) of our creative self–expression.

Signs on the Cusp of the Eighth House

The urge for personal transformation, the expression of our sexuality, and the other facets of the Eighth House are modified by the sign:

Aries with great urgency. This sign/house combination reveals a person who is ever searching for ways of personal transformation. This usually comes about in a highly confrontational manner—the individual must approach the conflicts of life head-on. Sexuality is a potent urge, usually demanding (but not always getting!) instant gratification. The person is responsible for the regeneration of his or her own resources, but has the courage, and creates the opportunities, to do so. This is a person who is not afraid to open new doors, release the past, and get on with his or her own life. Such individuals are also very supportive and encouraging of other people's crises of growth and development. Care has to be taken not to naively assume possession of the partners' resources. What is theirs may not necessarily be yours, and it is advisable to cultivate the patience that can determine the difference.

Taurus with a certain degree of resistance. This sign is exactly opposite the natural astrological ruler of this house, Scorpio. As such, its effects are polar opposites to the natural orientation of the house. Where Scorpio and the Eighth seek transformation and release, Taurus and the Second seek the status quo and increased physical manifestation. The results can be quite challenging, as the urge for evolutionary change may often be blocked through the misuse of one's willpower. In effect, the person can say: "I will not change!" Money from partnerships or other Eighth House sources may flow easily into her life. The individual will face challenge, in determining how to use these resources correctly. The central and recurring question will be: "How do I release and circulate my resources in order to bring greater benefits to myself and others?" Sexuality is usually experienced very profoundly, for the desire nature can be quite an intensely potent force in this sign/cusp combination. Longevity and an easy death are often promised.

Gemini as a talent for adjusting to the various changes in life. This is an individual who has a flexible attitude toward life's major challenges, one who "goes with the flow" and releases old patterns as life demands it. Life is a constant series of changes, and this person has learned (or will learn!) that the only constant in life is its inconsistency. Sexuality can fluctuate: Sometimes a person has long periods of sexual involvement, which may alternate with periods in which she is generally celibate. There may also be a tendency toward bisexuality, if other facets in the horoscope substantiate it. This person has no trouble working with other people's resources. In fact, such work may well be his or her profession, for this sign/cusp combination easily indicates a real estate agent, stock broker, bank teller, or similar occupation.

Cancer as the need to confront the past, especially one's family's attitudes towards sexuality and money. Whatever sign appears on the cusp of the Eighth speaks about the area of life that may most need to be transformed. As Cancer is linked to one's psychological foundations, or (as I like to call it) one's "biological karma," certain crises are found here. These crises create opportunities for release from certain subconscious family patterns of psychological conditioning, so that the true individuality may emerge. Money can come into one's life either through the partner's family or one's own efforts. Indeed, it may be through the family "purse strings" that the individual remains attached to the family "belly button." Once the necessary crises of transformation have been undergone, Cancer on the Eighth indicates a person who can be a nurturing presence for other people who are in the midst of deep psychological crises of personal growth.

Leo as the need to transform tendencies towards egocentricity. Human evolutionary growth results in the opening of the heart, a greater awareness of others, and an inclusivity in the way we think. Leo on the cusp of the Eighth enhances the personal passions. When the desire nature is stimulated by the fire of the Sun (Leo's ruling planet), one does not tend to see other people objectively, and this makes it hard to be truly heart-centered and helpful. As a consequence, this sign/cusp combination brings about lessons in the transformation of the lower self. Through the experiences of the broken heart, greater love can enter one's life. Once matured, Leo on the Eighth is a source of tremendous creative potential, applied to other people's resources. Leo on this cusp can stimulate creativity and increase the inherent wealth of both oneself and others on material as well as psychological levels.

Virgo through finding those techniques and processes that allow for healing and wholeness. This is fundamentally a very good sign/cusp combination. It gives a person the potential to transform and develop her natural talents and abilities.

Virgo on the Eighth indicates an orientation to refine oneself. One needs to perfect the desire nature, so that what is wanted for oneself is also helpful to others. On the other hand, this can give rise to a person who is very particular about her sexuality; in certain cases, this may reveal distinct fetishes or unusual sexual attractions and interests. This is a person who does well with other people's financial resources, and is usually very practical and discerning in this respect. It is an excellent indication for a bookkeeper, accountant, finance consultant, economist, or waste management controller.

Libra with a balanced sensibility. This sign/cusp combination has two distinct ways of expressing itself. On the one hand, Libra on the Eighth has an innate sense of tension. It knows exactly when the right time is to ask for a raise, make an agreement, launch the rocket, and release the status quo into another focus of expression. On the other hand, one may have great resistance to being the agent of any conflict. One may delay initiating the motion necessary to bring about needed changes (especially where relationships are concerned). The position of Venus will help the astrologer know which of these two directions is the more prevalent in the person's life. As a rule, this sign/cusp contact is very good for the use of other people's resources. There is a definite sense of fair play and a need to bring about harmony in all of one's financial dealings, especially when these involve one's love or business partner. Death usually comes about without violence, and often in peaceful surroundings.

Scorpio with amazing intensity. As this is the natural ruling sign of this house, there is no other sign/cusp combination that brings out the nature of the Eighth House more fully than this one. Sexuality and the transformation of the desire nature is a major theme of one's life. Scorpio in this position intensifies one's sexual orientation for good or ill, depending on the quality and level of the whole personality. This is, however, an excellent indication for a person who can work in one of the healing professions, for the ability to be transformative is very strong. Scorpio on the Eighth is an indication of a person who is a therapist, physician, or spiritual worker. As one would expect, money is also a very important issue. When negative, this is a person who can abuse other people's resources, and who can be most deceptive and dishonest. When positive, these individuals are a storehouse of ways and means, bringing about refinement and increase within the lives of themselves and others. As in all cases, whenever and wherever Scorpio is present, there is always a razor's edge, or a tightrope to walk. Death will either be an issue that comes with a great deal of foreboding and fear, or one of little consequence because the understanding of transition is so much an integrated part of the person's awareness.

Sagittarius with a philosophical attitude. Matters of death, life crises, and personal transformation are often approached with a sense of adventure. This is a person who may enjoy probing a more metaphysical approach to these issues. Sometimes this sign/cusp combination indicates that the very nature of a person's crises are rooted in his belief system. One comes to a point in life where one's religious background does not suffice for the situation at hand. This forces one to look elsewhere for the spiritual support that is needed. As a result, an expansion of one's beliefs comes about. In terms of one's sexuality, this can be an area of great openness and exploration, or one that may be circumscribed by a certain rigidity or orthodoxy of belief. The position of the Moon (family background) and Jupiter (the ruler of this sign) will have to be fully analyzed to determine which of these orientations are correct. Care may have to be taken that the individual is not too cavalier and wasteful of his own or other people's resources, for this is a position that can indicate a certain degree of self-indulgence.

Capricorn as a reserved or conservative attitude. This is a person who cares a great deal about finances and may be a very good source of information about how to increase one's wealth over time. There is usually a great deal of responsibility associated with the way one handles other people's money and this sign/cusp combination can indicate an investment counselor or even a banker. Sexuality is often restricted by this position. Sexuality seems, for many with Capricorn here, a normal part of one's life (which of course it is!), requiring no special emphasis. In some cases, however, Capricorn on the Eighth indicates a person who uses her sexuality as a tool to control or dominate others. In other instances, this is an astrological indication of a person who is sexually frustrated and restrained. The whole of the horoscope, and especially the position of Saturn (ruler of this sign), has to be examined to see which of these three is the natural tendency for the individual in question. Capricorn on the Eighth is frequently a sign of longevity as well as an indication of inherited wealth.

Aquarius as the urge for experimentation. This sign/cusp combination is often prone to investigate sexuality in ways that open oneself to new life experiences. There may be what most people would call, "peculiar" interests, or a certain openness and curiosity that goes beyond conventional attitudes toward sexuality. But, Aquarius is a very detached sign. Many people with this combination find that they are not particularly passionate, or may even have no interest in sexuality at all. (That lack of interest is itself rather unusual!) Aquarius on the Eighth indicates a person who likes to probe into the mysteries of life, and it is frequently found in the horoscopes of people with profound metaphysical and scientific orientations to life. From a financial perspective, Aquarius on the Eighth gives the tendency for "creative financing," and a penchant for finding new approaches to the use of other people's money. This position is especially interested in group endeavors and would incline strongly to investment in mutual funds, the stock market, and other financial outlets where many people are involved. For these individuals, one thing is certain: Their most profound life changes and crises will seem to come out of nowhere.

Pisces with connections to deeper psychological or spiritual issues. For most people, sexual expression is either a natural release of biological tensions, a result of the urge to procreate, or a means to express one's love for another being. Pisces on the Eighth experiences all of these but finds that sexuality is also a route of exploration into deeper and more subtle dynamics of the emotional nature. When this curiosity is objective, this is a very good sign/cusp combination for a psychologist, sexual therapist, or artist. If taken to extremes,

Pisces on this cusp can give rise to issues of sexual addiction and the need to lose oneself in sexual activity rather than the discovery of the more hidden and transcendent facets of one's nature. This combination is also a good indication for the renewal of financial resources, because Pisces is the sign that connects us to the collective bounty of the universe. Many people with this combination are never at a loss for money, because they are incredibly resourceful and often are in contact with organizations or individuals who provide powerful support. Yet it is important to keep in mind the dual nature of this sign and the dark waters and undercurrents of Neptune, planetary ruler of the Fish. With Pisces on the Eighth, a poorly placed Neptune in the chart can lead to financial deception and the misuse of one's own and others' resources.

Planets in the Eighth House

The Sun in the Eighth House acts as a catalyst or transformer in all life situations. This is a person who can bring about enormous, positive changes in other people's lives or be the vehicle for chaos. One is naturally aware of available resources, both financial and psychological, in one's relationships. There is a powerful urge to use such resources for mutual plans and projects.

The Moon in the Eighth House gives great sensitivity to changes and fluctuations in other people's emotional states. Someone with this position, which is excellent for the ability to "tune in" to other people's feelings, has a great capacity for subtle, emotional receptivity. What one *does* with this information—how one uses one's sensitivity—depends on one's level of maturity. In all cases, the Moon in this position links one's sexual drives very strongly to the emotional nature.

Mercury in the Eighth House indicates a mind that seeks to probe into the depth of things. This is a "spy mentality," which tends to uncover the hidden or more profound circumstances of any given situation. It may also indicate an individual whose thinking has a transformative effect on others.

Venus in the Eighth House can bestow financial benefits from wills, legacies, and marriage. It also indicates a person who may be highly skilled at transforming social situations, evoking greater creative possibilities within the scope of relationships. On the other hand, it can show a tendency to have at least one very challenging relationship, the results of which are extremely transformational in nature.

Mars in the Eighth House adds passion and intensity to the individual's sexual nature. If such energy is not modified, conflict and turmoil may result from a desire nature that is too strong. Mars in this position may also be a very helpful tool for supporting other people during crises, by adding courage and direction to their lives.

Jupiter in the Eighth House is an indication of abundant financial benefits coming from inheritance or partnership. If in poor relationship to the other planets, Jupiter can also reveal the tendency to squander and waste such good fortune. This is an individual who is greatly affected by religious and spiritual studies and beliefs.

Saturn in the Eighth House can create certain difficulties in the expression of one's sexuality. It usually has an inhibiting effect, or it can indicate a person who uses her sexuality to take control in partnership situations. Financially, Saturn here can help a person structure her resources for future growth and development. If poorly placed, it can mean the loss of inheritance or the necessity of taking on a partner's debt.

Uranus in the Eighth House is frequently an indication of unusual or erratic sexual behavior. There is a strong curiosity about sexuality and a distinct urge to experiment with different means of sexual self-expression. When Uranus is well placed, sudden and unexpected financial windfalls may occur through inheritances or relationship situations.

Neptune in the Eighth House indicates a very powerful dream life. This position increases psychic sensitivity and an interest in the fantastic. Certain unforeseen complications may occur regarding legacies and finances in general if Neptune is poorly placed here in relationship to the other planets. Sexuality can either be an incredibly uplifting facet of one's life, or an avenue for addiction and self-destruction.

Pluto in the Eighth House is a very potent placement, for Pluto is the natural ruler of this house. A person with this position can be a tremendous healing agent and a source of great renewal and regeneration. When this position is positive, amazing turns of events, which greatly increase one's financial position, may occur. When negative, Pluto in the Eighth House can transform sexuality into a very destructive life element.

Eighth House People, Places, and Things

Astrological Factors
> Quality: Succedent
> Quadrant: Southwest
> Natural Sign Ruler: Scorpio
> Natural Planetary Rulers: Pluto and Mars

B. People
> Coroners and undertakers
> Creditors
> Investment bankers
> Psychological therapists

C. Places and Things
> Crises of transformation
> Path of evolutionary development and growth
> Sexuality
> Sexual obsessions or illnesses
> Death, wills, legacies, alimonies
> Other people's resources (especially coming from partnership)
> Dreams
> Occult studies

I Am My Beliefs

The experiences of transformation, death, and release found in the Eighth House lead to the expansive dynamics of personal growth found in the Ninth. This is the astrological domicile of our philosophical and religious beliefs. The Third House is the container of our personal opinions—those thoughts and ideas that we communicate as our own. The Ninth opens us to the possibility of an increased state of awareness as it connects us to deep wisdom, higher knowledge, and the history of human thought. If we wished to have a map of our neighborhood, we would look for it in the Third House; if we wanted an atlas of the world, the Ninth is where it would be found.

The elementary school where our intellects were first stimulated and formulated is located in the Third House. The Ninth is the university where we expanded our mind and were given the opportunity to connect with the great minds of all traditions. The short journeys we made in childhood, which gave us a certain sense of independence, were accomplished through the Third; voyages of self-discovery that take us beyond the borders of our own nation, out of familiar places, are realized through the Ninth.

The Ninth is the house of collective knowledge—it is the encyclopedia of the horoscope. If you are a history buff, if your travel agency is an important part of your life, if you love to learn, then the Ninth House will be a very strong factor in your natal chart. This is also the house of moral values and social conduct. It is where we find the science of the law and where the Supreme Court of any nation is to be found. Lawyers are much more in the province of the Seventh House, for they act as arbitrators and administrators of the law. They fight either for or against you. But the Ninth is the house of eternal truths and, as such, transcends specific interpretations of how we are supposed to live and behave relative to our particular culture.

Signs on the Cusp of the Ninth House

The urge to expand the horizons of your life is modified in the Ninth House by the sign:

Aries as a deep need for personal adventure. As a rule, this sign/cusp combination gives the courage and stamina for long distance travel. It indicates a person who desires to find out who she or he experientially, facing the challenges of the road, air, or sea. Aries on the cusp of the Ninth points to a person who has an orientation for self-exploration. These people do not readily accept "higher truth," unless they can prove that such truth exists in terms of their personal encounters.

This person likes to chart his or her own course of studies, and does not embrace the status quo of higher education or moral conduct. Aries on the Ninth says, "I know, because I have proven what I know to myself."

Taurus as a strong urge to validate personal values by travel and higher education. Taurus wants things in life to be permanent. This is not a superficial sign: When placed on this cusp, it indicates a person who is looking for fundamental truths. Taurus on the Ninth may also indicate an individual whose educational aims are very practical. "I will spend the time, energy, and money necessary to further my knowledge," says this sign/house combination, "but I want to make sure that I can apply what I have learned, to earn a better living." This person does not like to leave the security and comforts of familiar territory in search of the adventures of life. Taurus on this cusp is quite content with a beautifully bound edition of the *Encyclopedia Britannica* in her library and a comfortable easy chair in which to study it.

Gemini as an avid curiosity and an eagerness to stimulate the mind. This is not, however, a fixed sign: Gemini on the Ninth tends to move from subject to subject, acquiring a broad knowledge rather than a particular specialty. People with this sign/cusp combination may be too quick to teach what they have just learned. There is a strong tendency to adopt a superficial approach to higher education. Travel is highly important, for there is a great need to acquire a wide assortment of experiences. These people may not be interested in undertaking a more profound exploration of the countries they visit. This is the kind of person who is more content visiting twelve countries in two weeks, than he is spending his entire trip getting to know one place well. One could say that Gemini on the cusp of the Ninth represents the tourist rather than the traveler.

Cancer as a need to anchor a fundamental sense of self. This sign/cusp combination is not noted for its urge for adventure. It indicates a person who needs to have the security of familiar surroundings. This is the traveler who will go to Ireland (for example) because he or she comes from Irish ancestry and is eager to make contact with his or her roots. Higher education is sought as a way to bring additional skills into one's life, so that one has more equipment for encounters with the world. Knowledge is cultivated as a protection against the unfamiliar, not for its own sake and not out of the mere love of knowing. If a special area of higher education is chosen, the choice is often made for deep, personal, and emotional reasons. Cancer on the Ninth points to an individual who tends to observe the family's religious traditions. This person may find great comfort and support in his or her ancestors' thoughts and feelings.

Leo as a great joy. Any cusp upon which the Lion appears is usually an area of life that is experienced with gusto. The Ninth is not an exception. This sign/cusp combination points to an individual who loves the adventures of life. Travel may be one of this person's favorite pastimes. He or she feels a deep sense of pleasure when surrounded by art, beauty, and lovely architecture. These people may take great pride in their journeys and be eager to share their experiences with others, for Leo loves to play "show and tell." Higher education is approached in much the same way—as a pleasurable adventure. Should the ego structure lack maturity, Leo on the Ninth will tend to indicate individuals who take too much pride in their personal knowledge. Their knowledge can be expressed with a tremendous self-centeredness and pomposity, which alienates and separates them from other people.

Virgo with distinct practical aims. Virgo collects tools, methods, processes, and techniques. When on the Ninth House cusp, this sign tends to seek out educational experiences that can widen its resourcefulness in the workaday world. This sign/cusp combination also points to a person who is constantly refining his or her knowledge. This individual is always at school, taking an extra course that may increase possibilities for advancement at work. She can be heavily critical and judgmental about religion and philosophy, especially those systems that seem too abstract and "other worldly." "I'll put what this philosopher or teacher says to the test," says Virgo on the Ninth, "and if it works out in a pragmatic sense, then I'll believe it." More spiritual people with Virgo on this cusp will use their knowledge, skills, or educational tools to serve others.

Libra as a means of meeting other people. This is not a sign/cusp combination for people who like to travel alone. Libra on the Ninth would rather sit at home than take a journey by herself. Companionship in the pursuit of the adventures of life or in the fulfillment of one's higher spiritual orientation is of the utmost importance. "I need to do this with a partner, if I am to have any real interest in the subject," says Libra on the Ninth. Art, music, and the law are three of the most natural areas of interest for study. In most cases, this is not an indica-tion of someone who is fanatically attached to some religion or philosophical belief system, yet, as in all things Libran, there is a balance. Some people with Libra on the cusp of the Ninth feel "married" to their beliefs and teachings and spend their entire lives perfecting their spiritual relationship to life.

Scorpio with very deep convictions. This sign/cusp combi-nation takes its beliefs and convictions seriously. Great trans-formative experiences come about in the areas indicated by Scorpio's placement in the chart. In the Ninth, crises of life orientation take place as a result of the individual's travels, higher education, spiritual beliefs, and general moral con-duct. This process revolves around the need to refine and redefine the personality through Ninth House subjects and concerns. A great deal of benefit can come to a person who is constantly involved with such challenges, for the results of such philosophical battles can improve the quality of life.

Sagittarius with enthusiasm and great interest. Sagittarius on the Ninth (its natural house) indicates a person who is especially eager to learn and to expand her or his horizons. Long-distance travels play a significant role and may be moti-vated by a desire for higher learning or religious or spiritual thirst. This sign/cusp combination embodies the philosophi-cal impulse, the ceaseless quest to know, and the fundamen-tal urge to grow through such experiences. The caution here is that the person may not construct the proper boundaries in his or her life. This is an individual who may set off from

Chicago to San Francisco, only to find that this trip takes her first to Paris!

Capricorn with a deep sense of responsibility. Expansion of one's education has to conform to an overall plan for life. This is not an indication of a person who loves knowledge for the sake of knowing. There is a definite reason for learning, a clear plan of endeavor, and a distinct goal in mind. Motivation for travel is similar: Capricorn on the Ninth points to a person who will travel to another city to attend an educational seminar that will enhance his or her career. The travel industry may be one's profession; one tends to organize other people's voyages or to be an administrator in a hotel or travel agency, rather than a guide to foreign lands. This sign/cusp combination lends itself to having a great respect for the past and a sincere interest in history and human cultural development. As a rule, there is very little spiritual exploration outside of one's inherited belief system or religion.

Aquarius with a great deal of experimental curiosity. This sign/cusp combination indicates an individual who is eager to explore the various beliefs of other cultures and people. A rebel when it comes to his or her own background, Aquarius on the Ninth often describes people who have stepped through the philosophical perimeters of their personal background in order to open themselves to new areas of experience. This is the Catholic girl from Boston who becomes a Buddhist, or the Jewish boy from New York who avidly explores various New Age beliefs and meditates at the full moon. On the other hand, Aquarius is a fixed sign. Depending on the rest of the horoscope, it may indicate someone with a firm sense of individuality, who belongs to no organized religion or organization and thinks of herself as a "religion of one."

Pisces with idealism, devotion, and sensitivity. This sign/cusp combination can give rise to a person who is very inclusive and who is accepting of all religious or spiritual beliefs. A true universalist, Pisces on the Ninth may find it very difficult to choose a particular field of study or spiritual path, preferring to remain unattached to one so that he or she may be attached to all. This is a very strong placement in the chart, for both Pisces and Sagittarius (the natural sign of this house) are governed by Jupiter, the natural planetary ruler of this house. Pisces therefore feels very much at home here, and gives rise to an individual who can be very devoted to his or her educational and/or philosophical pursuits. Travel is therefore a very important part of life, but voyages are usually undertaken as a form of retreat from the world, or as a means of acquiring some deep understanding about life. This sign/cusp combination is the embodiment of the spiritual journey and the Quest for the Holy Grail.

Planets in the Ninth House

The Sun in the Ninth gives the need to establish one's identity through life experiences that broaden one's scope of reality—travel, higher education, and spiritual pursuits. There is a need to be essentially free of those social situations which bind a person to a proscribed routine.

The Moon in the Ninth endows a person with a great sensitivity to what may be learned from traveling and higher education. This position indicates a certain restlessness and a great urge for an ever-changing environment. This is not an individual who will be happy staying at home, unless that home is in a foreign country or at a university.

Mercury in the Ninth urges one forward toward the expansion of one's mental horizons. There is an avid intellectual curiosity that promotes constant travel and/or educational experiences. This is not the most practical position for Mercury, for it indicates the mind of a philosopher who may easily develop into an "absent-minded professor."

Venus in the Ninth is often indicative of fortunate experiences that occur through travel or education. A scholarship may be offered, or a free ticket to attend a seminar. As the Ninth House is the third from the Seventh, this position may also indicate positive relationships with the partner's brothers and sisters.

Mars in the Ninth indicates a strong urge for adventure. If well placed in the chart, it can indicate a "spiritual warrior," someone who is ready to do battle or even die for his or her beliefs. If not in a positive sign or good relationship with the other planets, Mars in this house will bring conflicts in one's spiritual orientation and/or severe educational interruptions.

Jupiter in the Ninth is a very positive placement. It indicates a great deal of foreign travel and a profound interest in educational and philosophical pursuits. Legal issues are favored with this position, for Jupiter, if well situated in terms of the other planets in the chart, brings good fortune to any area where it is placed. Good judgment, and a comprehensive perspective on life, are other benefits that come with Jupiter in its own house.

Saturn in the Ninth may indicate difficulties with teachers and religious figures. The father may have sought to impose his beliefs and to choose one's course of education, which would have led to strife in the formative years. If Saturn is well placed in this house, one was blessed with excellent authority figures (teachers, a father, and older people in general) who greatly helped one choose the right path in life.

Uranus in the Ninth points to a person who is a natural rebel against established codes of belief and orthodox religions. This is an individual who was not well suited to an ordinary education and who may have had great difficulties adjusting to the norms of an established church or school. When well placed, this planet/house combination opens one to a wide variety of Ninth House experiences that add strength and character to one's individuality.

Neptune in the Ninth is often in the horoscopes of people interested in the mystical and the metaphysical. It typically has deep influence on one's religious beliefs, and may indicate a person who has either specialized in spiritual studies or one who received an education at a seminary or other form of parochial school. This planet/house combination can easily point to a person who gets lost in daydreams or in philosophical speculation.

Pluto in the Ninth brings profoundly transformational experiences through travel and/or education. This individual comes back, from a seminar or a foreign journey, either totally renewed or completely wiped out. Pluto knows no in-between—either you grow or you go! People with Pluto in the Ninth will usually change the religious or spiritual background from which they came or profoundly deepen their connection to their roots. The urge to uncover the deepest mysteries of life will certainly be present, along with the will-power to make such investigations a reality.

Ninth House People, Places, and Things

Astrological Factors
> Quality: Cadent
> Quadrant: Southwest
> Natural Sign Ruler: Sagittarius
> Natural Planetary Ruler: Jupiter

People
> Professors and scholars
> Ministers, priests, rabbis
> Metaphysicians and prophets
> Publishers
> Brothers and sisters-in-law
> Ambassadors and diplomats
> Judges

C. Places and Things

Foreign travel
Higher education
Philosophical or religious orientation
The science of the law (jurisprudence)
Law courts
Publishing
Orthodox religions and their institutions
Explorations and discoveries
University textbooks and research material
Foreign languages
World trade and commerce

The Tenth House

I Am My Profession

Second in importance only to the Ascendant/First House, the Tenth reveals the nature of one's career, overall potential contribution to society, and level of success in the material world. If the First House speaks about who you are, the Tenth tells what you may achieve as an individual. The Ascendant reveals potentiality while the Midheaven (cusp of the Tenth House) expresses the maturation and ripening of that potential. It shows the methods and means through which a person expresses his or her responsibility to the world, and it indicates the nature of the contribution one will make through a particular profession.

There is a very close and positive relationship between the Second House, the Sixth, and the Tenth. The Second speaks about our personal values, talents, abilities, and material resources. The Sixth House shows us how we handle the affairs of the Second House. In the Sixth, we acquire techniques, processes, and skills for putting our various abilities to best use. The Tenth shows how this interplay culminates in a defined career and place in society. The Tenth gathers together our potential and actual resources, integrates them with the processes that we have developed through our Sixth House jobs, and then synthesizes all of this into a cohesive package. Such as package might bear this identifying label: "This is my path of achievement in the world and my record of responsibility."

We also speak of the Tenth as the House of the Father, as it is the domicile of all authority figures that have played an important role in one's life—teachers, guides, employers, and older people in general. The Tenth is also the house of the government, and it reveals how an individual copes with society's rules and regulations, rulers and regulators. Please notice that the Tenth is opposite the Fourth, the House of the Mother. We could therefore say that the Fourth is the house of our "tribe," while the Tenth is the house of our "civilization." It is a much less personal house than the Fourth, which reveals so much about our psychological dynamics as anchored in our family roots. If the Fourth House cusp (the IC) represents our roots, then the Tenth House cusp (the MC) is the flowering of our fruits. If the roots have been well nourished, fed, and watered, then the tree of our being will produce abundantly. If the roots have been stunted, under-nourished, and abused, then an individual will have to struggle to produce in the world. A careful study of the relationship between these two houses is therefore very important to the astrology student.

Signs on the Cusp of the Tenth House (Midheaven)

A person's career and urge for achievement in life are modified in the Tenth House by the sign:

Aries as a need to be self-employed. This sign/cusp combination indicates a person who has to be the captain of his own ship. This tendency, if taken to the extreme, will leave a boat without a crew. It is therefore very important for this man or woman to learn to cooperate with others, so that mutual goals may be achieved. Aries on the Tenth shows that one is a self-starter who must master the technique of kindling her or his own creative spark. In a profession, the Ram on the MG needs constant challenges, new beginnings, and adventure. One brings courage, initiative, drive, and passion to whatever field one chooses. Common problems here are the tendency to begin more projects than one can finish, and loss of patience when events need to be highly structured in terms of time. The father was either a highly competitive man, with whom the individual fought many battles, or a very stimulating and supportive ally.

Taurus with an orientation towards the best use of one's abilities. These people seek to make the most out of what they have, but they may need to be more open to other people's input, if they would achieve greater success. On the Tenth, this very earthy sign indicates that financial achievement is an important goal; it will be a prime consideration in any career choice. Tenacity, strength of purpose, and determination come with the Bull on the MC but so does stubbornness and a resistance to change. Venus, the ruler of this sign, is

147

a positive influence that tends to bring abundance. Material considerations and personal security may, however, outweigh opportunities to shift careers. As a result, one may be stuck in a career that is financial rewarding but creatively stagnant. Affairs related to finance, real estate, and fine art are perfect avenues of professional expression. The father would typically be supportive and nurturing, but may tend to impose his values and opinions too strongly on the person's life path.

Gemini as a distinct need for variety and versatility. Writing, journalism, design, and work as an agent or intermediary are perfect outlets for this sign/cusp combination. It is most difficult for a person with the Twins on the MC to stay behind a desk, unless that desk has several phones, a couple of computer screens, and plenty of opportunities to communicate with others. Travel may also play a major part in the choice of one's career. Gemini is a dual sign: On this cusp, it can indicate that the person may be involved in more than one career at the same time. At the very least, there is an impatience with routine and with punching the clock. Restlessness is a common feature here. These individuals may constantly change their career focus or position. The father tends to have a strong mental nature, and may have been frequently away from home during one's youth. Gemini in this position may also speak about a parent who is much more intellectual than emotional in nature.

Cancer as an indication of one who has been highly influenced by his or her family. The mother is usually the dominant parent, when the Crab is on the Tenth. At the very least, the individual's career choices in life are deeply shaped by family background and traditions. Cancer on the cusp of the MC is ideally suited to all professions that involve nurturing. Such areas as food or hotel services, homes and real estate, working with children, and psychological counseling are perfect. If the individual has grown beyond the family roots, the orientation to nurture expands. These are people who feel that the world is their family and who may enter careers that are political in nature. In these positions, a person is able to administer social resources in order to feed, protect, and guide society at large.

Leo as a tendency to make a distinct personal mark in life. Leo brings strength, creative vitality, and potency to the Tenth House. It indicates a person who seeks to be noticed through his or her achievements and who is deeply determined to reach a high station, or at least a noticeable place, in life. This is a natural sign/cusp combination for a person involved in show business, the arts, and fashion. All leisure activities, and work having to do with young people in general, also come under the rulership of this sign. The Lion seeks to be at the center of his or her professional life and brings a great deal of verve and personality into the working environment. Sometimes the Lion roars—the tendency to become overly involved with oneself is a characteristic that can alienate co-workers and staff. The father of this person is usually loyal and faithful, but may also tend to be overbearing and dictatorial.

Virgo with attention to detail, and a thoroughly practical attitude. Work is at the center of one's life, when Virgo is on the MG. This person takes pride in her or his level of performance, and seeks nothing short of perfection in career achievements. Service has to play a major part in one's work ethic: It is vital for the Virgin to create opportunities for greater healing and wholeness when she rules the Tenth. This is a very positive position for people whose preferred work is supportive and helpful of others. The medical professions, various types of therapists, personal assistants, guides, and counselors are all favored by this sign/cusp combination. Money may be an issue of concern as there is a distinct need to be appreciated and rewarded when Virgo is on this cusp. The father tends to be a hard worker and quite pragmatic by nature. He may also be a highly critical person, who was not always easy to please.

Libra as an orientation to partnership. This sign/cusp combination points to an individual who seeks a career position that involves equal sharing of rewards and responsibilities. There is a tendency to want to have a relationship on personal and professional levels simultaneously, which can cause complications if certain boundaries are not observed. In any event, there is a genuinely friendly disposition and an urge to create rapports and alliances through the career. Yet this is also a highly competitive person, who is acutely aware that someone may court his or her position. Libra on the MC gives one an uncanny appreciation of other people's abilities and a natural talent for joining forces with such people, in order to minimize strife and maximize mutual benefits. The father is usually a friend and is very supportive; he is a man who may be gifted with charm and good looks.

Scorpio with an intense approach to success. This sign/cusp combination is often indicative of a person who will let no barrier stand in the way of his or her achievement. The direction of the Scorpion's power, when on the MC, depends deeply on the nature of the person's moral values (and on the natal position of Pluto, the ruler of this sign). Scorpio here can indicate a tremendously unscrupulous person, one who moves ahead through subterfuge and intrigue and eventually destroys himself. On the other hand, it may indicate someone, with equal tenacity of purpose and willpower, whose aims are transformational and uplifting. In this case, Scorpio on the Tenth reveals a person who brings new life into the professional sphere. This person can come into a failing business and, by uncovering and healing the company's weak spots, cause total renewal and regeneration. The father could be one's strongest support, contributing to one's courage and success; or he could be a very abusive parent. Scorpio is a sign of wide extremes!

Sagittarius with a constant focus on opportunities for advancement. "The sky's the limit" when the Centaur mounts the MC. Sagittarius on the cusp of the Tenth seems to be saying: "I see the goal; I reach it; and then I see another!" Although this optimistic attitude can be helpful in life, Sagittarius on this cusp may not look at the ground beneath his or her feet. Concentrating on the world of possibilities, one neglects to integrate what has already been achieved; therefore, one cannot build strong foundations. Nevertheless, this is usually a fortunate position, giving many opportunities to forge ahead. All professions involving sports, travel, teaching, and publishing are natural to this sign/cusp combination. The father is often a friendly sort of person. He may have held strong religious or philosophical beliefs, which either helped or hindered the individual. An examination of the position of Jupiter in the natal chart would clarify that issue for the astrological student.

Capricorn with strong ambitions and a great need for worldly success. This is the natural ruling sign of this house and, as such, is a very important and powerful influence. Typically, the Mountain Goat on the MC indicates a hard-working and determined person, one who envisions her or his personal peak of achievement early in life, and who works diligently to get there. The success that is desired, however, usually comes later in life. This often gives the individual a sense of being an underachiever, or of being held back by certain restrictions and obligations. Capricorn on the Tenth is a natural born administrator, CEO, ruler, and governor. He likes being in positions of respect and responsibility, and prefers giving orders to taking them. Some people with this sign/cusp position enjoy (or at least feel secure) being cogs in the wheel of such large organizations as international corporations or the bureaucracy of government. There is a need to feel assured that hard work over a long period of time will pay off with promotions. The father has the tendency to be dictatorial, rigid, and demanding, but if Saturn, ruler of this sign, is well placed in the chart, the father may instead be a wise patriarch.

Aquarius with a strong need for independence. This is a highly individualistic placement that points to a person who will not be happy in a career beset with predictability and routine. It is a sign/cusp combination that seeks a wide range of communicative possibilities, and it reveals a person who is heavily geared to working with computers and technological areas of self-expression. Aquarius on the MC also indicates a career involving organizations and groups composed of highly individualized people. This person needs to carve a distinctively personal niche in life—one's station must bear one's unmistakable mark. As this is an idealistic and humanitarian sign, the Water Bearer on the Tenth often indicates a man or woman who is involved in the political arena, and who seeks to create social change and improvements for humanity. The father may be emotionally distant and may have some very strong opinions about life—opinions which the individual disagreed with and challenged.

Pisces as the need to be of help to others. The Fish swim in waters of compassionate understanding and stimulate careers that serve to support and care for others. This is a very good indication of an individual who is in one of the healing professions. The arts are another area of natural interest. Pisces on the cusp of the Tenth is often an indication of a person involved in film, music, dance, and the arts in general. It is very important for the Fish to find her or his current, for it is easy for a person with this sign on the MC to lose him or herself in the many possibilities that life has to offer. Pisces always brings the urge for escapism. While the creative imagination may be highly stimulated by this sign/cusp combination, there is also a tendency toward distractions that keep a person away from personal success and achievements. The father can be a very spiritual and idealistic man, whose kindness and personal ethics contribute a great deal to the individual's character. If Neptune, ruler of this sign, is poorly positioned in the chart, the father may have problems with alcohol or be prone to other addictive forms of behavior.

Planets in the Tenth House

The Sun in the Tenth House gives the need to achieve a prominent position in life. There is the tendency to be very driven in one's pursuit of success, and there is usually no lack of personal ambition. The Sun is a powerful influence in this position, engendering a constant striving for some form of influence over others. It gives the need for power, but does not always bestow the ability to handle the responsibilities of power wisely.

The Moon in the Tenth House indicates that the person has an instinctual ability to feel the pulse of the general public. The career often involves reaching large numbers of people; more intimately, the urge to succeed is deeply connected with the need to nourish and take care of others. Personal and family situations often affect one's status in life.

Mercury in the Tenth House shows that writing, speaking, traveling, and communicating will play important parts in the individual's career. Sometimes public speaking is indicated, as well as some form of instructing. This is a clear indication of a person who is always "on the go."

Venus in the Tenth House can be most fortunate, for it gives the ability to. use one's considerable personal magnetism to add charisma to the professional life. There is a natural ease with people, accompanied by the urge to benefit others through one's social contacts. The arts and all careers that deal with beauty in some form are usually important areas of interest.

Mars in the Tenth House shows drive, determination, and ambition. Cooperation with others may have to be learned, for there is a distinct tendency to alienate anyone perceived as standing in the way of one's success. Conflicts with one's father and other authority figures may also be indicated by this position.

Jupiter in the Tenth House usually brings about some degree of prestige and professional success. There is a definite urge to expand upon one's achievements, refusing to settle for petty accomplishments. Travel, teaching, publishing, or a spiritual vocation are often indicated when Jupiter is in this position.

Saturn in the Tenth House can inhibit success, or it can bring a person into a more esteemed professional position—only after many years of hard work and effort have been expended. It is important to make friends with older people or those in superior positions, and to learn from their experiences. The father can be a major aid or a stumbling block, depending on how Saturn is positioned relative to the other planets in the chart.

Uranus in the Tenth House is an excellent position for a person who seeks an alternative lifestyle or a career that allows for a markedly distinct expression of individuality. Sometimes, it points to a person who is so rebellious and controversial that he or she is either defeated by society or obtains a high degree of notoriety. This is, for two reasons, an excellent position for an astrologer. Astrology is an "unusual" profession, and Uranus helps an individual to put a great deal of seemingly disparate data into clear categories.

Neptune in the Tenth House is an excellent position for careers that involve service to others, because this planet bestows a caring and compassionate nature. There is the ability to feel the collective suffering of humanity and (if other indications in the chart support it) the urge to relieve such pain through one's life work. Neptune in the Tenth is also very good for a career in the arts, for it highly stimulates the urge to project inner images and fantasy.

Pluto in the Tenth House is a very powerful placement. It can show that the individual will have several major professional crises, and if Pluto is well placed in the Tenth, it indicates that the individual will come out of such difficulties renewed, uplifted, and advanced. This planet/house combination also points to an individual with the capability to bring new life into any sphere of professional endeavor.

Tenth House People, Places, and Things

Astrological Factors
 Quality: Angular
 Quadrant: Southeast
 Natural Sign Ruler: Capricorn
 Natural Planetary Ruler: Saturn

People
 The father and all authority figures
 The partner's mother and family
 Kings, presidents, and all rulers
 Employers and business superiors
 Children of employees

Places and Things
 Career and profession
 Standing in society
 Relationship with authority figures
 Ability to adjust to social rules and regulations
 Governments and nations
 Death of brothers and sisters
 Money received as a result of long journeys
 Honors of notoriety
 Promotions or scandals leading to loss of social standing

The Eleventh House

I Am My Aspirations

Our astrological journey has so far taken us from the Ascendant (and its definition of who we are) to the Midheaven, where that identity is crystallized in terms of what we do in the world and the kinds of professional contribution we make. In effect, you have seen how all the component parts of yourself, as outlined in the first ten houses, integrate into the formation of a single, social entity—you!

When we travel through the last two houses of the horoscope, we enter into the sphere of life experience that takes us beyond the boundaries of our personal ego. The Eleventh House is specifically the domain of the collective entity known as "Humanity." In order to expand into an awareness of a universe beyond the borders of our ego, we have to identify with something greater than our little selves. We must move into an area of contact with life that allows us to assimilate new data, birth new life energies, and create new possibilities for our self-expression. The Tenth House and its planetary ruler, Saturn, reveal what we can become using the equipment of our own biological, psychological, and spiritual resources. The purpose of the Eleventh House and its planetary ruler, Uranus, is to let us know that we are more than what we think we are.

This process of unfolding our greater potential is connected with several areas of human interest and development that have their home in the Eleventh House. The first of these is the faculty of intuition, the sixth sense—that aspect of our awareness that lets us know the answer even before we hear the question. Intuition is under the influence of Uranus (the god of the skies, according to the ancient Greeks). The second way to enlarge our scope of being is through groups, organizations, and friends. These factors take us out of ourselves and into social situations that require us to engage with larger concepts and enhance our range of activities. All of these Eleventh House areas of participation enhance our growth and widen our perspective.

The Eleventh House is naturally associated with the element of air. Accordingly, it is involved with communication and relationships. The Third House speaks about mental abilities and our communication skills in general; it points also to relationships with our siblings and those friends who are as close to us as our brothers and sisters. The Seventh House tells us about our ways of communicating within intimate relationships and partnerships. The Eleventh House is much more impersonal in its attributes: It outlines our ways of communicating with society as a whole and with a more generalized and wide-ranging group of acquaintances and friends.

We have established our sense of self through our profession and career. The Tenth House has done its work. We now come into a time and place in life where we are free to take advantage of the resources that have come from our career and its experiences.[11] In this respect, the Eleventh House is also the place where we can see the area of hopes, wishes, and aspirations.

Signs on the Cusp of the Eleventh House

Your relationships with friends and groups of people, and the direction of your aspirations, are modified in the Eleventh House by the sign:

Aries with a need to further perfect the sense of self. The Eleventh House and all of its areas of interest will be of great importance to a person with the Ram on this cusp. This is an individual who has to prove himself in society. He does this by taking on leadership positions in groups and organizations. He stands firm to advance the cause of friends and associates. This person makes humanitarian, political, and social causes very much his own.

Taurus with a special concern for the material circumstances and consequences of one's social participation. This is a

---

11 The Eleventh is the second house from the Midheaven and this position indicates that it is the astrological domicile of the talents, abilities, and resources that come from Tenth House activities. Please see the last section entitled "The Secondary Meanings of the Houses" where these secondary house meanings are explained in fuller detail.

person who is very much at home being the treasurer of his club or organization. It is an individual whose aspirations in life are deeply connected to personal financial security and wellbeing. Taurus on the cusp of the Eleventh signifies a person who will be a loyal and faithful friend, steadfast and true to his friends and to the organizations of which he or she is a part.

Gemini as a tendency to have a wide set of acquaintances and a very active social life. This sign/cusp combination is highly favorable. It gives an individual the ability to get along with all kinds of people and to be especially instrumental in linking others together for mutual purposes. One should avoid getting involved with too many causes, having too many diverse loyalties, and becoming overly extended socially.

Cancer as the urge to be very protective where others are concerned. This is the sign of nurturance. When it is on the Eleventh House cusp, the Crab tends to be quite maternal towards friends and associates. This person tends to belong to charities and organizations that feed the poor and preserve the well-being of the planet. On the other hand, an emotionally immature person with this sign/cusp combination is apt to act very selfishly where others are concerned, because his or her aspirations are extremely self-protective.

Leo as the need to stand out in organizational activities. Leo likes to take center stage, but this orientation can bring conflicts in terms of group relationships. The hopes and wishes can be strongly egocentric, and the individual can feel that his or her aspirations and intentions are more important than the welfare and happiness of others. The Eleventh House serves to bring about equality, and the King or Queen of the zodiac wants to be treated royally! If the ego structure is mature, this is a great sign for dedicated leadership and supreme loyalty to others.

Virgo as a sincere urge to be of service to humanity, or to any organization of which one is a part. This is the person who volunteers to be the secretary or accountant of the group. It is also an individual whose eye for pragmatic details can be most helpful when in planning any financial situations involving groups or organizations. It is important for this sign/cusp combination to know that he or she has a defined place in any work that requires organization or in the lives of friends. Once so situated, Virgo on the Eleventh House cusp is an excellent position in the natal chart.

Libra as the urge to bring harmony into group dynamics. This is another excellent sign/cusp combination. It points to an individual with a need to share and be fair in all friendships and organizational relationships. This is a team worker, a person who knows that her own well-being is closely connected to the well-being of others. A difficulty that can come up with this position is indecisiveness. The person may have so many idealistic plans, hopes, and aspirations, connected to so many diverse people, that it can be a challenge to act with determination and drive.

Scorpio with persistence and intensity. This is an individual who is thoroughly fixed in his or her motives. This person can hold on forever to his or her hopes, wishes, aspirations, and visions. Even if life sounds a resounding call to change directions, this sign/cusp combination may insist on going ahead, no matter what the cost. This is not the most flexible influence when it comes to friendships and group dynamics. On the other hand, once a pledge of loyalty has been given, once a friend comes under his or her protection, once an agreement to a group has been made, Scorpio on the Eleventh tends to hold fast and firm.

Sagittarius with vision, idealism, and openness. This is a very good sign/cusp combination as both Sagittarius and Aquarius (the ruling sign of this house) are visionaries and idealists. The Centaur is on the Eleventh House cusp points to an individual who adds an amazing amount of energy and breadth of insight into any group function. Sagittarius is always looking at the larger picture, and avoids getting bogged down in petty egocentric disputes between friends or organizational workers. This sign embodies friendship and is always seeking out the positive in any form of relationship.

Capricorn with caution and reserve. The advantage of this sign/cusp combination is that it doesn't let hopes and wishes supersede the practicalities of life. This is a person who makes a good administrator, for he or she is willing to take on the responsibilities of leadership in any group situation. The difficulty associated with the Mountain Goat on the Eleventh House cusp is that personal ambitions and aspirations may get in the way of group orientation. There is also a tendency to hold a group back, due to one's own sense of personal restrictions.

Aquarius with a natural urge to participate in collective goals and aspirations. Aquarius is the natural ruler of this house and, as such, its placement here tends to be quite positive. This sign/cusp combination is very much at home in group settings. One tends to be able to merge one's own aspirations with those of friends and larger groups of associates. If supported by other indications in the chart, the Water Bearer on the Eleventh House cusp indicates a personality willing to be supportive of others, a team player, and a person who places other people's welfare on at least the same level as his or her own.

Pisces with a very sympathetic and compassionate world view. As the most universal of all the signs, the Fish is strongly predisposed to support those groups and organizations that seek to be of service to humanity and the planet. At times this urge may tend to the extreme, and it is then that an individual with this sign/cusp combination can lose his individuality within a group context. When the self-sacrificial urge of the Fish is too great, this person can feel that she or he is easily taken advantage of by friends or by people in general. Pisces on this cusp can also indicate a person with very strong spiritually and metaphysically oriented interests and friends.

Planets in the Eleventh House

The Sun in the Eleventh House indicates that one has a strong need to integrate oneself into a larger social collective. This position can easily indicate someone with an interest in public welfare, who finds that groups and organizations will play a significant role in one's life.

The Moon in the Eleventh House can greatly stimulate one's intuition about people. There is a tendency to have many different kinds of friends—people from all walks of life and different social backgrounds. Friendships are highly important, and relationships of all kinds are cultivated and nurtured.

Mercury in the Eleventh House points to the tendency for an intensely active life. This person moves around a great deal socially and has a wide range of friends and interests. There is a need to communicate on a large variety of subjects, and an ease with using those technological tools that make such communication possible.

Venus in the Eleventh House indicates gain and benefit through associations and friends. It can also indicate that the individual has a wide range of love interests and many romantic experiences. The degree of fulfillment of one's hopes, wishes, and aspirations is closely connected to the quality and nature of one's personal relationships.

Mars in the Eleventh House can be a troublesome position, for there is a tendency to use one's friends and associates to further personal goals and aspirations. Conflicts within groups and organizations are likely, if one has not learned how to integrate one's own desires with the wishes of the collective. If Mars is well placed in this house, it can be a highly useful tool for furthering the ambitions of friends, and of the group to which one belongs.

Jupiter in the Eleventh House brings a great deal of good fortune from friendships and from one's group affiliations.

This person is likely to participate in some socially oriented spiritual group, such as the Masons or the Shriners. This is a person who enjoys social life and takes great pleasure in being among, and traveling with, friends. This planet/house combination also indicates a person who wants to share his group's beliefs with a wide range of people.

Saturn in the Eleventh House gives the tendency to have older or well-positioned friends in life. As Saturn is the natural co-ruler of this house, he feels very much at home here. Yet this position can be troublesome if Saturn is "stodgy" and insists that the traditions of the past inhibit the more forward-moving ideas and aspirations of one's group of friends. It is a positive placement when such previous experiences serve as a platform for tomorrow, and when the individual adds his or her understanding of life to collective plans and projects.

Uranus in the Eleventh House is a powerful placement, for it is the natural planetary ruler of this house. There is a great many opportunities for sharing visions and concepts with various groups of people. This planet/house combination indicates a person with a wide range of friends, an individual who is unafraid to challenge the status quo of his or her society or culture. Uranus in this position is highly experimental socially—it leads one into many different, possibly quite unusual, social experiences.

Neptune in the Eleventh House often indicates that discrimination is required in one's choice of friends. If afflicted, Neptune in this position points to people who are dishonest, self-abusive, and addicted to various harmful activities and substances. When well placed in the Eleventh, there is a tendency to join religious and spiritual groups that support a deep urge to love and serve all people regardless of race or life orientation. Artistically, this position of Neptune is very good for participation in all forms of entertainment groups, especially those that deal with film, music, or dance.

Pluto in the Eleventh House can indicate the disappearance of friends who, many years later, resurface in one's life. It also indicates the ability to be an intense transformative agent in group circumstances. This planet/house position can reveal a person who is able to bring new life and direction into the collective goals of any group or organization. Pluto in the Eleventh often acts as a "devil's advocate" in social situations, stirring up what may be negative and hidden, thereby bringing to the surface new creative possibilities for all concerned.

Eleventh House People, Places and Things

A. Astrological Factors
Quality: Succedent
Quadrant: Southeast
Natural Sign Ruler: Aquarius
Natural Planetary Ruler: Uranus and Saturn

B. People
Friends and acquaintances
Members of groups and organizations to which one
    belongs
Stepchildren
Senators, members of the House of Representatives
Spouses or partners of one's children
Astronomers
Social workers, humanitarians, social scientists
Bohemians, eccentrics, revolutionaries
Geniuses

C. Places and Things
Groups and organizations
Fraternities and sororities
Society in general
Hopes, wishes, aspirations
Resources from one's profession
Father's resources
Computers, communication satellites
The Worldwide Web and the Internet generally

The Twelfth House

I Am the Universe

This is the most mysterious house of the horoscope and the least personal. If you move through the houses in their natural direction, the Twelfth is the farthest from the Ascendant. The message and meaning of the First House—"I Am Myself"—is very far removed from the message of this house, the last of the astrological domiciles: "I Am the Universe." To think of each of us being the universe is quite far removed from our daily concerns over family, friends, money, lovers, children, career, and the like.

Yet if we keep traveling just one more step in this same direction, the Twelfth will lead us immediately back to the First House. This is the horoscope's way of telling us: "Yes, as hard as it is to conceive, each of us is a universe unto ourselves." This is the fundamental principle of astrology at work—"As above, so below." Astrology can help each of us find his or her place in life, because this ancient science reveals that you and I are reflections of the Whole. As we grow in our awareness, and as we individualize and evolve, we find that our sense of ourselves as separate units (the Ascendant) gradually gives way to a much greater consciousness of the Cosmos in which we live and breath and have our being.

The Twelfth House is the custodian of this truth. It is the most occult, the most esoteric, the most spiritual of all houses. If we believe in reincarnation, the Twelfth can be said to be the "House of Karma" as it reveals what is stored from previous "turns around the wheel." It is therefore the house of our secret treasures and strengths, our hidden resources, and even our guardian angels. The last house of the natal chart contains all the power and potency of all the good we have done—and this, after all, is our karma and our inner reserve of "luck."

But there is another side to ourselves, to our karma, and to the nature of the Twelfth House. It is also the place of our self-undoing, that part of our nature which is self-destructive and harmful. Locked away with our hidden resources, lie our (not entirely) hidden weaknesses. Right next door to our protective devas live our worst enemies. Side by side with that facet of our personal karma, which brings us good fortune and absolute protection, is that aspect of ourselves which can be the most harmful of all. The Twelfth is the house of monasteries and convents, but it is also the house of insane asylums and dungeons. The Twelfth is where hospitals, hospices, and hope may be found, but it is also the place in the chart where jails, slave quarters, and despair are located. The great healing plants, herbs, and wonder drugs are in the Twelfth House, but in the next drawer are to be found heroin, crack cocaine, and all other addictive, life-destroying substances.

The amazing duality of the Twelfth House is most confusing to astrology students. How can our greatest weakness become our greatest strength? How can our addictions lead us to rebirth and renewal? How can the path to our spiritual reality be found in the same house with the path to our self-destruction? The Twelfth House, like the nature of life itself, is full of such puzzling questions. It also holds the answers.

No matter what we may believe about past lives, the Twelfth House reveals what we need to overcome in this one. It also tells us a great deal about the power we possess deep within ourselves to help us accomplish the tasks of life. Once we leave the Twelfth, we return to the Ascendant and the First House. If we have managed to clean out the unwanted elements of the Twelfth and externalized the light within us, when we next get to the Ascendant we can say: "I am healed and I am whole. I Am Myself and the Universe."

Signs on the Cusp of the Twelfth House

The nature of the more hidden facets of our life, and of our orientation to self-healing or self-undoing, is expressed in the Twelfth House through:

Aries as an urge to mask or suppress personal assertiveness. This is an individual who functions best when behind the scenes. On a positive level, this sign/cusp combination can make for a good strategist, whose real power, though far from obvious, is definitely present. When negative, this position leads to self-denial and self-victimization. A Ram likes to charge forward unimpeded, but finds the Twelfth to be difficult terrain for his direct and forthcoming tactics. This is an excellent placement, however, for a person happier to be the power behind the throne than to occupy a visible position of authority.

Taurus with a tremendous reserve of power. The Bull on this cusp is one of the more positive sign/cusp influences, for it allows an individual to have a secret storehouse of talents, abilities, and riches for use when life is at its most difficult. It is also a position that indicates a wealth of common sense and the ability to stand fast under pressure. Problems arise if one's attitude to money is not correct. It is then that difficulties come into life through illegal use, or mere mishandling, of funds. When used wisely, Taurus on the Twelfth is a potent source of supply, for this position indicates a very resourceful person who is definitely open to "universal supply."

Gemini as a natural tendency to duality. This is a person who can write his name on the blackboard with his right hand while simultaneously erasing it with his left! Here, the left hand doesn't always know what the right hand is doing. One has to be very careful that there is consistency and honesty in all forms of communication; otherwise, definite confusion will arise. Gemini on the Twelfth can try to be all things to all people and lose himself in the process. If the rest of the horoscope reveals a certain maturity of character and a more steadfast nature, this is a wonderful position for being able to find the "missing links" in all social situations. It indicates a person who can find the missing fax, locate a long lost friend, and say just the right thing at the right time, to resolve conflicts and disputes.

Cancer as a need to help and protect those in distress. Here, it is most important to relax and let the universe do the work. This sign/cusp combination has the tendency to become too personally involved in caring for those in need—attachment occurs, when detachment is most needed. There are few other zodiacal positions that contain so much potentiality for nurturance and compassion as this one. It gives the tendency to mother everyone, but the spiritual food and source of that orientation has to come from the universal storehouse. Unlocking the key to this abundance is a very important aspect of this individual's spiritual path.

Leo as a challenge to integrating personal creative impulses with a spiritual perspective. Leo demands, wherever it is placed in the chart, that this particular part of one's life stand forward and be noticed. But the Twelfth House is the most subtle and least noticeable of all. This sign/cusp combination accordingly brings forth lessons of humility and quiet service. Leo on the Twelfth indicates an immense wealth of potent willpower, yet the will is not allowed to be used in obvious ways. This can lead to a very manipulative person, one who works through subterfuge and deceit to get his or her own way. The fiery potential of the Lion can be a potent source of support and stimulus for others. In turn, this generous activity brings greater strength, healing, and power into one's own life.

Virgo with a distinct orientation to healing and wholeness. This position indicates a person who has the practical know-how, skills, and techniques to be of assistance whenever it is needed. It leads to a natural urge to work with people in hospitals and institutions, where help and sustained support is required. This sign/cusp combination allows one to bring order out of chaos, but this can only happen if the individual has an integrated personality. If such is not the case, this can be a most challenging position. To find the cure for everyone, and a place for every minute detail of life, is an amazingly difficult task. Care has to be taken here not to lose the thread and get tangled up in the spool.

Libra in the way one shares one's life in relationships. This position sometimes makes it difficult to see the level of intimacy that is required in our dealings with others. Sometimes one is too detached and, at other times, the depth of connection is not at all warranted by the situation. There is the tendency to be too idealistic, not seeing people for who they really are. The spiritual gifts of this position are very profound: They can lead to a universal and unprejudiced way of loving and sharing oneself. The darker side of this sign/cusp combination has to do with improper, clandestine relationships, and becoming involved with people who have neither their own nor the other person's best interests at heart.

Scorpio by the tests of our desires. Although the potentiality for great emotional growth and spiritual development is very strong with this position, so are the dangers and pitfalls. Scorpio on the Twelfth House cusp requires one to be very clear about the direction of one's needs and wants. If this orientation is undisciplined, the individual is a ceaseless fount of unquenchable desires. Yet if the lessons of this trap have been learned and successfully integrated into one's nature, no position has a greater power for healing. One is then able to find within oneself the "universal catalyst"—that aspect of life which, when released, uplifts and brings wholeness to all who allow themselves to receive it.

Sagittarius with a profound need to unlock the doors to universal truth. This sign/cusp combination often points to an individual with a deep interest in the metaphysical and the philosophical. It is a person on a constant quest for knowing. Although this is, in itself, a very positive orientation, it can give rise to a type of restlessness that denies inner peace. What is required here is the discipline of remaining one-pointed on one's path in life; Sagittarius is known to bring about many distractions. On a more practical level, this position allows a person to come up with information he never knew he had. This quixotic ability to know obscure facts or, at the very least, to have a clear understanding where such information may be found, is also indicated when the Centaur rides the Twelfth House cusp.

Capricorn with a need to understand the inner structure behind outer events. This sign/cusp combination indicates a person who must understand who holds the real power in any social situation. One is made acutely uncomfortable by the thought that one's personal power or influence may be suppressed by individuals or circumstances beyond one's immediate control. As a result, this can be a highly manipulative position. On the other hand, the Mountain Goat on the Twelfth can be a rich source of hidden wealth and resources. It may indicate a person who has mastered the art of giving directions and structuring life situations, to the extent that this skill is available to all who have need of it. It also can point to an individual who has great powers of organization, so subtle in her execution that her influence is barely perceptible. If the whole of the personality is well intended, this characteristic makes for an accomplished, and devoted teacher and a very benevolent leader.

Aquarius as an idealistic and humanitarian nature. This is a person who knows people! It is a man or woman to whom no life situation seems strange, and for whom no one is a stranger. This person senses clearly the universal stream of life running through each and every one of us. This position brings a challenge. The individual must not get lost in the currents of the compassionate water he carries. There is a distinct tendency towards diffusion, when this sign/cusp combination is present. So many directions are accessible, so many possibilities for relationship present themselves, so many doors through which one may enter in order to serve are open, that it is extraordinarily difficult for this person to choose. Discernment and discrimination are, therefore, two qualities that may have to be integrated into one's life.

Pisces as a distinct attraction to the universal waters of life. This attraction has many benefits and dangers. As the natural ruler of this cusp, Pisces on the Twelfth can indicate a person with an extremely deep spirituality, an inner calling to "come home" to the source of all life. These feelings often lead one to a path of great inclusivity and compassion. Yet if one has little understanding about the depth of the ocean, and the play of its tides and currents, one can drown even with the most noble of intentions. The urge to free oneself from the responsibilities of earthly life may be very strong, leading to addictions of all kinds, including blind devotion to "spiritual" cults. The Fish can swim either upstream to undreamed of harbors of enlightened service to humanity, or downstream into oblivion.

Planets in the Twelfth House

The Sun in the Twelfth House frequently places one in positions which are behind the scenes and out of the public eye. There is a strong need for seclusion and privacy and a deep inner resourcefulness. Typically, one's creative potential is not discovered until later in life, for the vision of one's own individuality may be obscured, or difficult to discern.

The Moon in the Twelfth House speaks about a person with a great many mixed feelings and emotional cross-currents. It is a man or woman who is in close touch with how others experience their lives but who may have a difficult time individualizing her or his own emotions. Sometimes this sensitivity is so strong that long periods of solitude are required. This is an excellent placement for the Moon, when one is involved in any of the healing or therapeutic professions.

Mercury in the Twelfth House gives a large scope of vision and ease at communicating all sorts of generalized ideas and opinions. The challenge, for these people, is to be able to state their own minds and their own views of things. Breadth and depth of thought are present, rather than precision and logic.

Venus in the Twelfth House is often an indication of a person who has many hidden relationships. There is a tendency to be deeply secretive about one's personal involvements. There is certainly a high degree of compassion and understanding for others, but there can also be a lack of discrimination about one's involvements in other people's lives. This lack of clarity can give rise to many interpersonal complications. Artistic interests and talents may be important influences in one's life, and there is usually a certain degree of protection or secrecy where money is concerned.

Mars in the Twelfth House can be quite secretive—one may obscure one's real motivation for action. This tendency can give rise to a person who bottles up anger and aggression, and who is quite reluctant to reveal his or her true intentions. This person is likely to be passively aggressive, or simply unaware of the urge to manipulate circumstances. Hidden enemies can be a problem. This is someone who may easily antagonize others, without being fully conscious of doing so. On a more positive level, Mars in the Twelfth is a good strategist. This person can be counted on to find the resources needed to get himself, or anyone else, out of a difficult situation.

Jupiter in the Twelfth House is an indicator of protection. A most positive placement for Jupiter gives access here to both spiritual and material resources, especially in times of need. Care has to be taken not to waste, and not to spend, what one cannot afford to lose. The danger of this position is carelessness and overestimation of possibilities. In general, however, this is a most agreeable and fortunate influence to have in one's chart.

Saturn in the Twelfth House usually indicates certain hidden fears. Quite often these are connected with problems with one's father or authority figures in general. There is often a reluctance to assume personal responsibilities and an anxiety over personal failure. If Saturn is well placed in the Twelfth, this is an excellent position for one involved in serious research projects. It may also give the constant support of a teacher or older person whom one consults as an advisor and guide.

Uranus in the Twelfth House adds the gift of intuition to one's nature. If Uranus is not well situated in this house relative to the other planets, it can point to a person who doesn't pay attention to the inner voice, and harms him or herself accordingly. It is an excellent placement for behind-the-scenes social networking, such as occurs in the organization of charitable or humanitarian functions.

Neptune in the Twelfth House can be a highly difficult placement, as there is the tendency to undercut one's own support and bring some intensely harmful situations into one's life. A tendency to deceit, dishonesty, and addiction is also noted. But, should Neptune be well positioned relative to the rest of the chart, this is a most wonderful placement. In this case, Neptune yields a deep spiritual understanding of life, along with a profound sense of compassion and an awareness of other people's true needs.

Pluto in the Twelfth House can annihilate any potential harm that threatens one's life. It also gives an enormous opportunity to uncover hidden treasure—in people, finances, or one's spiritual life. Pluto is the god of the underworld and as such it is connected to gold, silver, and diamond mines. But he also rules sewers and swamps. A poorly placed Pluto in this house is a clear warning to beware of underworld people, such as gangsters and other criminals.

Twelfth House People, Places, and Things

A. Astrological Factors
Quality: Succedent
Quadrant: Southeast
Natural Sign Ruler: Pisces
Natural Planetary Ruler: Jupiter and Neptune

B. People
Secret enemies
Secret friends
Clandestine lovers
Guardian angels
Captives, prisoners, slaves
Spiritual teachers and gurus
Monks and nuns
Prostitutes and pimps
Gangsters and criminals
Drug traffickers and drug addicts
Psychics and mediums

C. Places and Things

The path to one's self-undoing
The path to one's spiritual renewal
The hidden shadows
The hidden treasures
Inner weaknesses
Inner strengths
Partner's health
Partner's job
Things that are lost
Prisons, asylums
Hospitals, hospices
Secret societies
Karma
Metaphysical and spiritual study, research and investigation
Meditation

The Secondary Meanings
of the Houses

Everything that we do here on earth can be found in the houses of the horoscope. Even astronauts and rocket ships can be found in the houses. (Look in the Ninth, house of explorers and long journeys!) The list of all the people, places, and things that belong to these twelve sections of the natal chart would take volumes and volumes, for astrology does indeed measure the full extent of human activity.

It is necessary help for the reader to develop his or her "astrological mind." Astrology is a science but it is also an art: The art lies in the ability to interpret a chart that has been calculated scientifically. It is up to the astrology student to learn to locate anything and everything in the natal chart. This understanding unfolds with time and practice. What I would like to present, in this final chapter of Houses of the Horoscope, is a guide that will enable you to find whatever you are looking for, within the astrological domiciles.

You need only know the keywords and concepts of the houses, and remember their numerical sequence from one to twelve. Some examples will follow these keywords—and then there will be a brief "test." After a bit of study, you will be able to find in your own chart the house pertinent to your mother's sister's pet cat! (I'll give you the answer on page 188.)

First House: Me, myself, and I.

Second House: Resources (primarily, but not entirely, financial), values.

Third House: Communication, siblings and very close friends, short journeys, primary and secondary education.

Fourth House: Family (primarily one's mother); psychological foundations, endings, home.

Fifth House: Children, creative self-expression, romance, leisure, and fun.

Sixth House: Tools, methods, techniques of self-improvement, work, health, pets, employees.

Seventh House: Marriage, committed partnerships (both business and romantic); open enemies, competitors.

Eighth House: Sex, death, wills and legacies, other people's resources.

Ninth House: Long journeys, higher education, religion and philosophy, publishing.

Tenth House: Father, authority figures in one's life, standing in society, career and profession.

Eleventh House: Hopes, wishes, aspirations, groups and organizations, friends, society in general.

Twelfth House: Hidden resources, "karma," self-undoing, unseen benefactors, secret enemies.

Sample Test

1.   Example: In which house in your horoscope would you find your children's partners?

Answer: The Eleventh—the Eleventh House is the seventh house (partners) from the Fifth (children).

2.   Example: In which house in your horoscope would you find your sister's money?

Answer: The Fourth—the Fourth is the second (money) from the Third (siblings).

3.   Example: In which house in your horoscope would you find your sister's husband?

Answer: The Ninth—the Ninth is the seventh house (partners) from the Third (siblings).

4.   Example: In which house in your horoscope would you find your sister's husband's money?

Answer: The Tenth—the Tenth is the second house (money) from the Ninth (sibling's partners).

Now, as for your mother's sister's pet cat, that little creature would be found in your Eleventh House. First you go to the Fourth House to find your mother. Next you look at the Sixth House to find her sister (the Sixth House is the third from the Fourth). Finally, you go to the Eleventh House as it is the sixth house (pets) from the Sixth.

A Little Test

See how well you are thinking "astro-logically." Where would you look in your chart to find the following?:[12]

1. Your college professor's home.

2. The nature of cooperative links with other organizations to the organizations to which you belong.

3. Your partner's religious or philosophical beliefs.

4. Your mother's health.

5. Your grandchildren.

6. The outcome of secret negotiations.

Your personal universe is found within all the houses of your horoscope. I hope that this book will be of help in finding it.

---

12 The answers are found on page 190

ANSWERS TO ASTROLOGICAL HOUSES TEST:

1. **The Twelfth.** The Twelfth is the fourth house (homes) from the Ninth (college teachers).

2. **The Fifth.** The Fifth is the seventh house (partners, cooperative ventures) from the Eleventh (organizations).

3. **The Third.** The Third is the seventh (partners) from the Ninth (philosophy and religion).

4. **The Ninth.** The Ninth is the sixth (health) from the Fourth (mother).

5. **The Ninth.** The Ninth is the fifth (children) from the Fifth (children).

6. **The Third.** The Third is the fourth (endings) from the Twelfth (behind-the-scenes activities).

Reference Guide

The following books will add to your understanding of the astrological houses.

Bills, Rex E. *The Rulership Book*. Macoy Publishing: Richmond, VA, 1971.

Lehman, J. Lee. *The Book of Rulerships*. Whitford Press: West Chester, PA, 1992.

McEvers, Joan and March, Marion. *The Only Way to Learn Astrology, Vol. 3*. Astro Computing Services: San Diego, CA, 1982.

Oken, Alan. *Alan Oken's Complete Astrology*. Ibis Press, Lake Worth, FL, 2006

Oken, Alan. *Rulers of the Horoscope*. Ibis Press, Lake Worth, FL, 2008

Oken, Alan. *Soul-Centered Astrology*. Ibis Press, Lake Worth, FL, 2008

Sasportas, Howard. *The Twelve Houses*. Thorsons: London, 1985.

IBIS PRESS

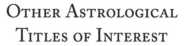

OTHER ASTROLOGICAL
TITLES OF INTEREST

Tracy Marks
*Art of Chart Interpretation—A Step-by-Step Method of Analyzing,
Synthesizing & Understanding the Birth Chart*
2008   ISBN: 978-0-89254-142-3   192 pp   Price: $16.95

Tracy Marks
*Astrology and Self-Discovery—An In-Depth Exploration of
the Potentials Revealed in Your Birth Chart*
2008   ISBN: 978-0-89254-136-2   320 pp   Price: S18.95

Jackie Slevin
*Finding Success in the Horoscope—The Slevin System of Chart
Analysis*
2008   ISBN: 978-0-89254-141-6   208 pp   Price: $18.95

Demetra George
*Astrology and the Authentic Self—Integrating Traditional and
Modern Astrology to Uncover the Essence of the Birth Chart*
2008   ISBN: 978-0-89254149-2   320pp   Price: $24.95

Demetra George and Douglas Bloch
*Astrology For Yourself—How to Understand and Interpret Your Own
Birth Chart: A Workbook for Personal Transformation*
2006   ISBN: 978-0-89254-122-5   272 pp   Price: 19.95

Demetra George and Douglas Bloch
*Asteroid Goddesses: The Mythology, Psychology, and Astrology of the
Re-Emerging Feminine*
2003   ISBN: 978-0-89254-082-2   368 pp   Price: $22.95